OSPREY
MILITARY | CAM

TEL EL-KEBIR 1882

GENERAL EDITOR DAVID G. CHANDLER

OSPREY MILITARY

CAMPAIGN SERIES

27

TEL EL-KEBIR 1882

WOLSELEY'S
CONQUEST OF EGYPT

DONALD FEATHERSTONE

◀ *Lieutenant-General Sir Garnet Wolseley, Commander-In-Chief of the Army in Egypt 1882.*

First published in Great Britain in
1993 by OSPREY, an imprint of Reed
Consumer Books Limited, Michelin
House, 81 Fulham Road, London
SW3 6RB and Aukland, Melbourne,
Singapore and Toronto.

ISBN 1-85532-335-4

Produced by DAG Publications Ltd
for Osprey Publishing Ltd. Colour
bird's eye view illustrations by Peter
Harper. Cartography by Micromap.
Mono camerawork by M&E Repro-
ductions, North Fambridge, Essex.
Printed and bound in Hong Kong.

▶ *At Kassassin on 9
September. A general
view of the action and
field, by a 'special artist'
of* The Illustrated
London News. *The
extent of the background
is about four miles; in the
right-hand background
an enemy shell bursts in
the British camp. In the
centre background clouds
of smoke indicate the
position of British 25pdrs.
The artillery in the centre
are Borrodaile's Battery
RHA; beyond them, four
squadrons of Bengal
Lancers are riding for-
ward to meet the enemy,
who are outside the limits
of this sketch.*

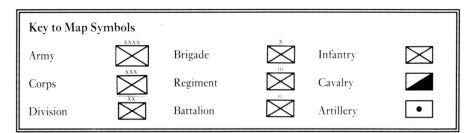

Key to Map Symbols

Army	XXXX	Brigade	X	Infantry	
Corps	XXX	Regiment	III	Cavalry	
Division	XX	Battalion	II	Artillery	

CONTENTS

INTRODUCTION – HISTORY REPEATS ITSELF

When, in 1882, Lieutenant-General Sir Garnet Wolseley led a British military expedition to Egypt, fought and deposed the dictator Arabi Pasha and restored the country to the Khedive, it foreshadowed events of exactly one hundred years later when a British task force went out to the Falkland Islands, conquered the troops of an Argentinian dictator, Galtieri, and returned the islands to British sover-

eignty. Separated by a century, both armies left with emotional dockside farewells, and returned to Victory processions through London and public investitures by their respective Queens - all in best Victorian style.

The Egyptian War of 1882 and the South Atlantic Campaign of 1982 have much in common and bear some remarkable similarities, not the least

The Nile Delta in 1882

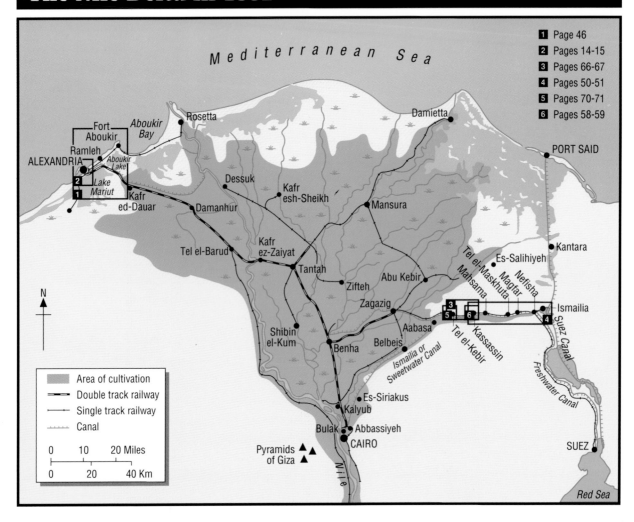

1 Page 46
2 Pages 14-15
3 Pages 66-67
4 Pages 50-51
5 Pages 70-71
6 Pages 58-59

Legend:
- Area of cultivation
- Double track railway
- Single track railway
- Canal

0 10 20 Miles
0 20 40 Km

being that, from the moment of landing until the cessation of hostilities, both lasted exactly 4½ weeks. Both stretched the resources of the British Army, causing each expedition to be formed of 'crack' Regular regiments not normally used for such purposes.

Somewhat bitterly, and in a markedly ironic tone, *The London Illustrated News* (July 1882) commented upon this in a leading article:

'England as a Great Power. Of course, we are incontestably one of the Great Powers, and yet it is pretty certain that Spain, which would like to have been present at the Constantinople Conference, but was shy of asking for fear of a rebuff, could more easily spare a respectable military contingent for foreign service than we can. Of course, we are a Great Power, and we are actually going to strengthen the Mediterranean Fleet by sending out a thousand Marines. A thousand Marines! Think of that Arabi, and tremble in your sandals. There is talk too of bringing Sepoys from India, should fighting appear likely, and precedents are being industriously cited to justify such a course. Yes, England is a Great Power, but it is a fact, sad or auspicious, according to whether it is regarded from the Jingo or the Wilfred Lawson point of view, that England has very few soldiers to spare. Half our Regular Army of 190,000 men is in India and the colonies, and the lion's share of the remainder is in Ireland. Says the *United Services Gazette*, "We could not, without the undue strain of calling up our Reserves, muster more than 16,500 men of all arms for active service, and of this force a further contingent will be required to prevent Ireland from taking advantage of our embarrassment. England could not place more than 15,000 men in the field without denuding her colonies, and leaving her magazines and arsenals unprotected from those desperadoes who deal in dynamite." Our contemporary recommends the addition of 10,000 men to the Royal Irish Constabulary, so as to relieve an equivalent body of troops. In case blows should be exchanged, it is lucky for us, seeing that as regards military force we are such a Lilliputian Great Power, that the Turkish officers, who had practical trial of Egyptian troops during the late war with Russia, have no very exalted opinion of them.'

Strikes a familiar modern chord, doesn't it?

Overture in Egypt

It began in 1862, when the Khedive Ismail came to the throne of Egypt and immediately embarked upon a programme of public works and improvements with complete disregard of cost. Building railways, harbours, telegraph systems and many other modern amenities, he transformed Alexandria and Cairo while greatly improving the country's agriculture and commerce. But these brilliant achievements bankrupted and ruined the State, oppressing the people with an insupportable burden, until bond-holders and creditors began to be alarmed about the capacity of the Treasury to provide the huge sums required for interest. Money provided by European capitalists had to be repaid through charges on the country's revenue, which itself depended upon the Egyptian Government's direction of its own transactions. The Nationalists accused the Khedive of 'pawning' his country through being forced to accept European direction of its affairs.

As creditor for a great proportion of Egypt's debts and with more extensive commercial relations than those enjoyed by other countries, England inevitably played a prominent part in the direction of Egyptian affairs. On top of that, seeing the Suez Canal as an essential highway to India, in 1875 Great Britain had emphasized its presence by acquiring nine-twentieths of the shares in the waterway. Subsequent concessions made by the Khedive in 1878 amounted to almost complete surrender, arousing belief that British and French influence would so guide Egyptian counsels that the country's involved finances would be put straight.

But this obvious European domination, supported by the Egyptian Prime Minister, and the sudden dismissal of numerous Egyptian Army officers and Civil Servants, caused demonstrations and serious riots. The Khedive, aware that his own Prime Minister and the British Minister of Finance in Egypt were determined to reduce him to a mere figurehead, came into active opposition to the government that had been forced upon him. In June 1879 the diplomatic representatives of Britain and France jointly advised the Khedive to abdicate in favour of his son Tewfik; at which the Sultan of Turkey, who held sovereignty over Egypt, deposed

▲ *Tewfik Pasha, Khedive of Egypt during the time of the Arabi rebellion. Coming to power in 1879, when Britain and France had advised his father to abdicate in his favour, he found himself unable to stand up to Arabi and his followers, but subsequent events in Egypt up to and including Kitchener's Omdurman campaign of 1896-8 allowed him maintain his position in Egypt.*

Ismail and replaced him by Tewfik. The former Khedive, with sons Hussein and Hassan, his harem and a large suite, embarked for Naples, and his 27-year-old successor took over the Government.

The Rise of Arabi

The new Khedive began with an honesty of purpose, and by 1881 his genuine attempts at reform indicated promise of progress, but he lacked the authority of will to tackle undeniable grievances among his military leaders. Precipitated by ill-feeling between Arab and Circassian officers, the army mutinied in mid 1881, under the leadership of Arabi Bey (Said Ahmed Arabi), a middle-aged man of tall stature, exceptional eloquence and a some-

what imposing presence. He had joined the army while still a boy, and was a recognized leader among his fellows even before his promotion from private soldier to commissioned rank. His persistent agitation and insubordination caused him to be cashiered, but he was soon reinstated by the Khedive, and was promoted to the colonelcy of a regiment. It soon became evident that Arabi had the charisma to be the natural leader of the lower ranks while at the same time representing the temper of the majority of the officers. In September 1881 a military revolt led to a confrontation before the Royal Palace in Cairo, between the Khedive and a group of Arabi-led Colonels; subsequently their demands led to Arabi's appointment as Minister of War early in 1882.

Since the very inception of formed armies, soldiers have shown that they will do anything for a commander who shows self-reliance, decision and strength of mind – and it was these qualities that account for Arabi's great influence over his countrymen. Unwavering, he boldly pursued his objective, entirely regardless of obstacles, and in defiance of those European nations hitherto regarded as the arbiters of Egyptian destinies. At the time of the outbreak of war, Arabi had achieved unqualified success – he had forced the Khedive to keep him at the head of affairs; he had endeavoured to wrest internal power from the hands of Europeans, only to see the balance restored by the aggressive action of the British fleet. At that time he was not only countenanced by the Sultan of Turkey, who was both his spiritual and secular leader, but that same ruler had bestowed upon him one of the highest Ottoman decorations – at a time when the ambassadors of the great European powers were taking counsel together in Constantinople as to the best means of overthrowing him!

The rise of Arabi alarmed both British and French Governments, who jointly addressed a Note to the Khedive, informing him of each country's intention to, 'ward off by united efforts all causes of internal or external complications which might menace the regime established in Egypt'. This meant, of course, that both countries intended to maintain their joint control for the good of Egypt, the peace of Europe, and the benefit of Egypt's European bond-holders and creditors. Both

Governments puzzled over an effectual type of intervention should Egypt tumble into anarchy – England had strong objections to occupying Egypt by itself as it would create opposition in that country and in Turkey, besides exciting the suspicion and jealousy of European powers, possibly leading to demonstrations and serious complications. A joint occupation was not a happy solution, so perhaps the least objectionable course might be a temporary Turkish occupation – under proper guarantees and controls.

During the next few weeks the matter was given a good airing in the British press and the public awaited events with interest. During this period a temporary understanding between the Khedive and his Minister of War appeared to cool the situation and, in March 1882, Arabi was made a Pasha. He immediately assumed the role of dictator, while the Khedive made futile endeavours to contest his activities. London newspapers talked of 'the grave political anxieties... and the dubious position of the Khedive's government'. In early April a plot against Arabi's life was discovered, planned by Circassian officers in the Egyptian Army who were arrested and court-martialled, receiving the severest sentences. Early in May Arabi's followers were infuriated when the Khedive commuted these to mere exile. Arabi's inflamed supporters uttered wild threats, including a general massacre of foreigners in Egypt.

Yet only a week later the British press was displaying a surprising optimism, stating: '... the Egyptian crisis is over... British and French naval squadrons are in readiness at Suda Bay in Crete, but there is no immediate intention of landing troops in Egypt. But a week later it was reported that the British Naval squadron had moved to Alexandria, 'as it is considered that the crisis is at its most critical point'.

There were reports that Arabi was emplacing guns at Alexandria and Damietta, and that he had 'laid torpedoes'. During the next few weeks it was reported that the Egyptian populace were being stirred-up by foreign interference, and that a crusade was being preached against foreigners, particularly Europeans. On 17 June the situation boiled over and rioting was reported in Alexandria, some Europeans being killed in wild attacks directed at foreigners and their properties. Eventually Egyptian

▲ *Arabi Pasha, the Egyptian Minister for War, leader of the Nationalist Party, and commander of the Egyptian forces during the war of 1882.*

troops entered the city to quell the rioting and restore order; foreigners were advised to leave, but there was a shortage of shipping for a mass evacuation.

In Britain the Press reported that the new Egyptian leaders were hostile to Britain and France, and that their appointments merely placed Arabi in a stronger position, able to excite disturbances that threatened every European settled in Egypt; Arabi was a troublesome conspirator and order in Egypt could never be restored until he was removed from office.

Melodramas need a villain and over the centuries British wars have spawned a notable selection – Hitler, the Kaiser, Napoleon, Cronje, the Mahdi and the Khalifa, Cetewayo, Tippoo Sahib, the Rani of Jhansi, and in 1982 the Argentian Galtieri, and his counterpart a century earlier – Arabi Pasha, the Egyptian Minister of War. Of him, *The Illustrated London News* said:

'Suddenly arises a military adventurer with a peculiar audacity and cunning such as Oriental races can alone produce, who has been able, step by step and in the face of a wondering world, to establish, without let or hindrance and out of the most contemptible materials, a military despotism which threatens to depose the Khedive, and which defies, with impunity, the Western Powers and their iron-clad fleets.'

Britain, alive to the fact that a crisis confronted her, displayed misgivings, doubts and justifications for seeking to protect interests in Egypt, and it was not generally thought possible that Britain would, or could, mount an expedition to go to Egypt. All possible steps were taken to settle without fighting; intense and prolonged diplomatic activity sought a peaceful solution, simultaneous with steps of an obvious military nature to pressure the Egyptians into compliance. When military operations eventually began, there was much foreign antagonism and criticism, and France, Britain's sole ally in Egypt at that time, suddenly and dramatically reversed her policy of support.

The war came about through a mixture of causes. The common factors were pride, financial interests and the maintenance of Britain's interests in Egypt, not least the Suez Canal. The Egyptian War really began early in 1882 with a whimper, the Press stoking the fires by regular references to demands, grievances, protestations and stances of the antagonists, causing them to smoulder, fanned by assiduous man-made breezes, until finally bursting into flame. The British public played a major role, revealing archetypal Victorian fervour and patriotism, indicating that their esteem needed a British military victory. But not all were in favour of war, as was shown by fierce Parliamentary opposition, and pacific protests by such as Sir Wilfred Lawson's Anti-Aggression League, the Peace Society, and the Working Man's Peace Association.

▼ *The rioting in Alexandria on Sunday 11 June 1882. After two hours, troops appeared at about 5 p.m. and charged* *the mob, which rapidly fled, leaving the streets under military control.*

▶ *The fortifications at Alexandria. A Krupp field-gun in a newly erected earthwork. The sentry is Egyptian, but the officers may well be Turkish as were many artillery officers.*

Meanwhile the impassioned demands of Arabi that the foreigner be driven out of Egypt brought thousands to his banner; as a European Power, Great Britain could not submit to his authority and demands. In early June 1882 Britain found that she had drifted into fighting for the Khedive against his own Minister of War. Despite the presence of the Mediterranean Fleet, lying in harbour at Alexandria, rioting and the massacre of Christians continued in the city. Arabi, growing bolder each day, boasted that the forces at his command could hold the city against the fleets of all Europe. His trained engineers worked frantically to strengthen the shore forts and to throw up new earthworks in which they mounted heavy guns. So blatant was this work that, on the morning of 10 July, Admiral Sir Beauchamp Paget Seymour issued an ultimatum

that either the forts be surrendered or they would be bombarded. Arabi's reply indicated that he chose the bombardment, and the British ships cleared for action.

The Bombardment of the Forts at Alexandria

For weeks the British sailors aboard the ships of the Mediterranean Fleet had suffered disappointment and frustration as they lay under the shadow of the great forts, awaiting the signal-gun that would tell them to open fire. Typically, they had christened their enemy 'Horrible Pasha' and they could hardly wait to get at him – now it seemed the time had come as they stood in silence, stripped to their flannel jerseys, hoping against hope. Half-past six and the guns remained silent, a quarter to seven and no

command given – then, ten minutes later, loudly and unexpectedly, the battleship *Alexandra* fired a shell at the Pharos Fort and the bombardment had begun.

This is the report our great-grandfathers read in *The Illustrated London News* of 15 July 1882:

'On Tuesday morning, 11 July, after several weeks of anxious suspense, the attempts to bring about a peaceful settlement of the Egyptian difficulties were interrupted by a terrible conflict between the forts and batteries at Alexandria, under command of Arabi Pasha, and the British Naval squadron commanded by Admiral Sir Beauchamp Seymour, occasioned by the Egyptians' conduct in persisting against repeated prohibitions, to continue their defensive and offensive warlike preparations. The Admiral had discovered on Sunday, that there were two new guns mounted on the western side of the entrance to the harbour, whereupon he prepared a proclamation to be posted up, charging the Egyptian authorities with breach of faith, and demanding the surrender of the fortifications within twelve hours. If this were not complied with he would fire on them after another twenty-four hours. There being no sign of a disposition on Arabi's part to surrender, the bombardment was begun at seven o'clock on Tuesday morning. It is said that a launch was met at daybreak, with another deputation coming to promise that the fortification works would be stopped and the guns dismounted, but the Admiral replied that it was too late.'

Alexandria had two distinct systems of defence: one protected the New Fort and Eastern Town, the other, dominated by Fort Pharos and Fort Ada, protected the entrances to the Outer Western Harbour. Admiral Seymour planned to deploy his squadron in such a way as to be able to bombard all the

▲ *Earthworks and batteries erected 600 yards from HMS* Monarch *in the harbour at Alexandria; they would be of little use during hostilities because the men in the batteries were exposed to the ships' Gatling and Nordenfelt machine-guns.*

▶ *Above right: the Lighthouse Fort at the entrance to the harbour had a large, fortified barracks for 2,000 men. The guns of this fort were second-rate weapons, mostly cast-iron, smooth-bore 64pdrs, with a few rifled guns; it was considered that a single ship could dispose of these fortifications.*

▶ *Panoramic view of Alexandria, from outside the harbour, looking east.*

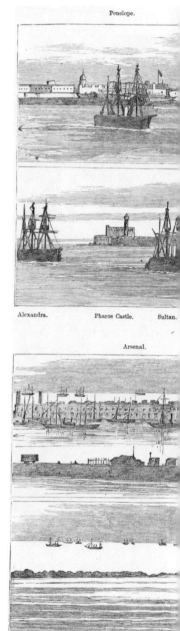

Penelope.

Alexandra.   Pharos Castle.   Sultan.

Arsenal.

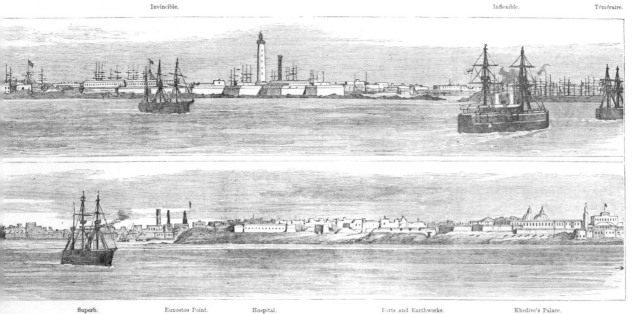

Invincible.   Inflexible.   Téméraire.

Superb.   Eunostos Point.   Hospital.   Forts and Earthworks.   Khedive's Palace.

PANORAMIC VIEW OF ALEXANDRIA FROM OUTSIDE THE HARBOUR, LOOKING EAST.

Inner Harbour.   Quays.

Alexandria was considered a first-class sea fortress, with nearly 250 guns, but the defences were old and the artillery was of mixed value. However, the British ammunition performed poorly, more than half of the shells failing to burst, exploding prematurely or splitting on impact. (Most ammunition aboard the ships was armour-piercing and unsuitable for shore bombardment.) And nearly all the ships suffered damage caused by their own guns.

Technical information based on Oscar Parkes, *British Battleships 1860–1950*, Seeley, Service & Co, London, 1957.

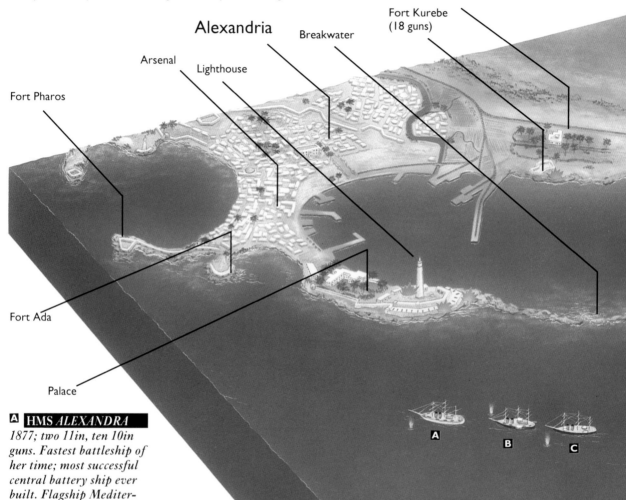

Alexandria

Fort Pharos

Arsenal

Lighthouse

Breakwater

Gabbari Palace

Fort Kurebe (18 guns)

Fort Ada

Palace

A HMS *ALEXANDRA*
1877; two 11in, ten 10in guns. Fastest battleship of her time; most successful central battery ship ever built. Flagship Mediterranean Fleet. Fired 48 11in and 221 10in shells.

B HMS *SULTAN*
1871; eight 10in, four 9in guns. Reinforced Mediterranean Fleet from the Channel Fleet.

C HMS *SUPERB*
1880; sixteen 10in guns. Had largest battery of single-calibre guns ever mounted in a British battleship and fired the heaviest broadside of any British battleship to date.

D HMS *INFLEXIBLE*
1881; four 16in guns. Extraordinary ship with turrets en echelon and carrying the heaviest guns in the Royal Navy. A milestone in battleship design, precursor of central citadel ships and with underwater armour deck instead of vertical

[Continued at top right]

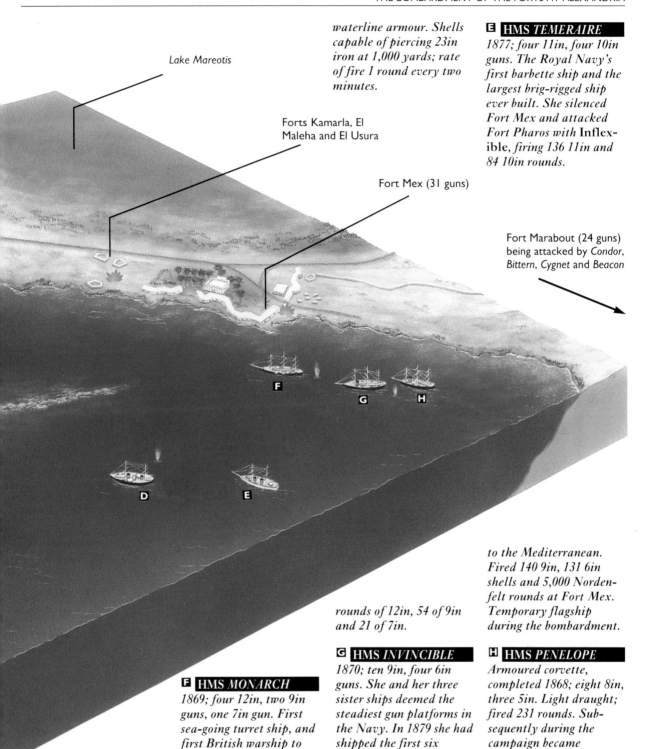

Lake Mareotis

waterline armour. Shells capable of piercing 23in iron at 1,000 yards; rate of fire 1 round every two minutes.

Forts Kamarla, El Maleha and El Usura

E HMS *TEMERAIRE*
*1877; four 11in, four 10in guns. The Royal Navy's first barbette ship and the largest brig-rigged ship ever built. She silenced Fort Mex and attacked Fort Pharos with **Inflexible**, firing 136 11in and 84 10in rounds.*

Fort Mex (31 guns)

Fort Marabout (24 guns) being attacked by *Condor*, *Bittern*, *Cygnet* and *Beacon*

to the Mediterranean. Fired 140 9in, 131 6in shells and 5,000 Nordenfelt rounds at Fort Mex. Temporary flagship during the bombardment.

rounds of 12in, 54 of 9in and 21 of 7in.

G HMS *INVINCIBLE*
1870; ten 9in, four 6in guns. She and her three sister ships deemed the steadiest gun platforms in the Navy. In 1879 she had shipped the first six Nordenfelt guns supplied

H HMS *PENELOPE*
Armoured corvette, completed 1868; eight 8in, three 5in. Light draught; fired 231 rounds. Subsequently during the campaign became flagship in Suez Canal.

F HMS *MONARCH*
1869; four 12in, two 9in guns, one 7in gun. First sea-going turret ship, and first British warship to carry 12in guns. Fired 125

THE BOMBARDMENT OF ALEXANDRIA

11 July 1882, as seen from the north, the last action in which a British battle fleet fought with muzzle-loading guns and the first in which it was protected by armour

Egyptian positions simultaneously. The French squadron and other foreign vessels had left the harbour on the previous day; all was clear for action.

The British fleet consisted of eight ironclads, supported by five gunboats. All the ships were fully manned and, in addition to their heavy armament, most of them were fitted with torpedoes and machine-guns of the modern Nordenfelt and Gatling patterns. The Squadron was under the command of Vice-Admiral Sir Frederick Beauchamp Paget Seymour, GCB, Flag Officer Mediterranean Station. He hoisted his flag in *Invincible* which, with *Monarch* and *Penelope* (*Temeraire* remaining on hand outside the harbour), took up positions commanding the entrance to the harbour, almost opposite Meks and 1,000–1,300 yards north-west of Fort Marsa el-Kanat on the mainland shore. They engaged these forts while

◀ *This sketch by the war artist Melton Prior depicts the crew of a Nordenfelt machine-gun, protected by a rampart of hammocks on the upper deck, preparing to open fire on the Egyptian gunners in the embrasures of the shore battery.*

▶ *Sketches of various aspects of the action, by special war artists of* **The Illustrated London News.** *From top to bottom: Fort Ada, blown up by* **Superb,** *and the magazine behind Barrack Fort, blown up by* **Alexandra;** *the fight at its hottest, south of the Lighthouse Battery; the meeting of* **Alexandra** *and other ships after the action; the damage inflicted upon Lighthouse Tower; and a shot hole through a funnel on* **Alexandra.**

▲ *The respective positions of the warships off the Lighthouse Fort, and their targets ashore.*

◀ *This drawing by Melton Prior, made aboard HMS* Alexandra *during the attack, shows the working of the 10in broadside guns (port side).*

▶ *Another sketch made aboard* Alexandra *by Melton Prior: a shell from a shore battery hits the vessel. Her hull was struck by 25 missiles. During the action one man was killed and two wounded.*

Superb, *Sultan* and *Alexandra* engaged and totally destroyed the Lighthouse and Pharos forts. *Inflexible* co-operated with both divisions from her position commanding the Lighthouse and Pharos batteries, and Fort Meks.

At close range the five gunboats engaged the Marabout batteries at the entrance of the harbour and soon silenced them, after which they ran in and shelled Fort Meks; *Bittern* covering a landing-party from *Invincible* which blew up the heavy guns in that fort. The Egyptians fought their batteries with more determination than had been anticipated, but by 4 p.m. all had falllen silent; four had been blown up, and the Khedive's palace was on fire.

The bombardment ceased at half-past five, when it was reported that five men had been killed and 28 wounded; the wounds mostly caused by splinters when solid shot penetrated inboard, the Egyptians apparently having no explosive shells. The casualties among the Egyptians must have been very great, but we are unable to obtain any idea of their number. As soon as firing had ceased Admiral Seymour sent ashore twelve officers and men who made their way to the ruined forts and destroyed the guns with dynamite.

On Wednesday morning, as had been planned, Forts Napoleon and Gabarrie, and the inner harbour batteries, were engaged by *Invincible*, with

▲ *HMS* Sultan *off Ras-el-Tin, or Lighthouse Fort, at Alexandria, July 1882.*

◀ Inflexible *(in the foreground) with other vessels in action in the background. Her 16in guns played a prominent part in the action, one of their huge shells dismounting a 10in gun in one of the Egyptian batteries, turning it end-over-end, and killing the entire crew.*

Monarch and *Penelope* which had entered the inner harbour the previous evening. *Invincible* silenced the batteries, then landed a party which spiked and burst nine guns. Towards noon *Inflexible* and *Temeraire* opened fire on the Moncrieff battery outside the harbour, which had been repaired during the night. The battery did not reply. The Khedive's

▼ *Commanded by Lord Charles Beresford (right), HMS* Condor *energetically engaged the Marabout Forts at the western extremity of the Bay of Alexandria.*

This 774-ton gunboat was armed with one 4½-ton, one 7½in calibre and two 64pdr guns; her complement was 100 men.

▼ *Interior of the Egyptian Lighthouse Port after the action had ceased.*

◀ *With fires still burning in the city after the bombardment, the British naval landing party pull towards the shore. In the background is the Khedive's palace.*

◀ *The naval landing-party marching up the Marina in Alexandria, drawing a Gardner gun.*

▼ *Two sketches by Melton Prior. Below left: the execution by a naval firing party of an Arab incendiary caught in the act in the streets of Alexandria. Below right: the arrest of one of Arabi's spies by Royal Naval police at the Moharrem Bey Gate in Alexandria.*

palace was still burning, and there were other fires in the town. The wind had risen and there was a sea swell which made manoeuvring in the confines of the harbour difficult.

But at one o'clock the signal 'Cease Firing' was hoisted in the Admiral's flagship outside the breakwater. A white flag had been flown in the town, signalling the desire for a truce. The Admiral sent a gunboat, with a white flag at the fore, up the Inner Harbour to the Arsenal wherein were the official residences of the Ministers of War and of Marine. 'At the time of writing this, on Wednesday evening, nothing more is known; but we may hope that a suspension of hostilities is already arranged.'

The British Expeditionary Force

It had been thought that the naval action at Alexandria would be enough to destroy Arabi and restore the Khedive's authority, and for some time Cairo and the rest of Egypt remained quiet, watching events. When it was seen that the British apparently were content to remain inactive within the confines of Alexandria, belief in the star of Arabi revived and the entire nation again threw in its lot with him. Had the Government in London immediately dispatched a force to march against Arabi, there can be little doubt that they would easily have defeated his dispirited army, but British reluctance to commence open warfare gave the Egyptian leader time to regain lost prestige. He withdrew his troops to what became a strongly fortified position, brought up heavy artillery and increased the size of his army. Thus emboldened, he issued a proclamation declaring that, 'irreconcilable war existed between the Egyptians and the English'.

The British Government was still far from united on Egyptian policy and, while other European powers were not unsympathetic towards the bombardment of Alexandria, they were quite unwilling to give Britain an explicit mandate – France would only co-operate with Britain in defence of the Suez Canal and became increasingly hostile to intervention of any kind. Nevertheless, the powers did not interfere and so British policy, practically unfettered and, with public opinion and the press in jingoistic mood, settled upon the dispatch of an expeditionary force to secure British interests in Egypt. The War

Office and the Admiralty acted with unusual energy and promptitude, and on 25 July the Queen signed the Proclamation calling out the Army Reserves; two days later the first of them, including Royal

Seaman of the Naval Brigade. The sennet hat bears the ship's name on a tally band. The rifle is the Martini-Henry with cutlass bayonet. (G. A. Embleton)

Expeditionary Force to Egypt

From Britain:	Officers	Men
Cavalry	118	2,174
Artillery	56	1,514
Engineers	30	876
Infantry	270	6,958
Medical, Transport and		
Commissariat Branches	38	1,384
Total	512	12,906

(Nominal force according to the Official Return)

From Malta:
1st Bn South Staffordshire Regiment
3rd Bn King's Royal Rifle Corps
1st Bn Berkshire Regiment
1st Bn Gordon Highlanders
2nd Bn Manchester Regiment
Four Companies 1st Bn Sussex Regiment

From Gibraltar to Malta and then on to Egypt:
2nd Bn Duke of Cornwall's Light Infantry

From Gibraltar:
1st Bn Cameron Highlanders
2nd Bn Derbyshire Regiment

From Cyprus:
HQ and four Companies
1st Bn Sussex Regiment

From Aden:
1st Bn Seaforth Highlanders

From Bombay:
1st Bn Manchester Regiment

Total: 40,560 officers and men

◄ *The Scots Guards under their Brigade Commander, HRH The Duke of Connaught, marched from Wellington Barracks to Westminster Pier in London on 28 July, to embark in three river-steamers for Albert Dock.*

Marines, sailed from Portsmouth. Before the end of the month the Guards had left London, and by 15 August two divisions, each of two brigades of infantry, with cavalry and artillery, were on their way. A Staff Corps composed of the three squadrons of the Household Cavalry, two regiments of Dragoons, with artillery and a siege-train, commissariat, transport, and medical department, was dispatched from Britain.

The total of all troops from Britain, the Mediterranean and India was 40,560 officers and men of all ranks.

THE OPPOSING COMMANDERS

The British Commanders

Well known in British military history and a leading 'trouble-shooter' of the Victorian period was Lieutenant-General Sir Garnet Wolseley, GCB, GCMG, commander of the British force. Born near Dublin in 1833, he entered the army as an ensign in 1852 and saw service in the Burmese War of 1852–3; he distinguished himself in the Crimea and was severely wounded at Sevastopol. Later he gained great distinction during the Indian Mutiny and the China War; in 1870 he commanded the Red River Expedition in Canada, and led the expedition to quell the Ashanti in 1873, for which achievement he was created GCMG and KCB and received an award of £25,000. Appointed Governor of Natal in 1874, and then High Commissioner in Cyprus in 1878, in the following year he was sent out to replace Lord Chelmsford as commander of the British forces engaged in the Zulu War, but the war ended before he could take over.

Promoted to Quartermaster-General and then Adjutant-General in 1880, his plans for the re-organization of the army were interrupted when he was ordered to Egypt to command the expeditionary force. After the successful outcome of the war in Egypt, Wolseley commanded the expedition that was sent to the Sudan in 1884 to extract Gordon from Khartoum. After a period commanding the British Forces in Ireland, he was promoted to field marshal in 1894. An intelligent and far-sighted soldier, he sought constantly to improve the image of the British soldier and to forge the army into an efficient instrument of war.

Chief of Staff and second-in-command of the army in Egypt, Lieutenant-General Sir John Adye, KCB, was born in 1819. An artilleryman, he was present at many of the major Crimean War battles, and went on to take an active part during and after the Indian Mutiny. He served with distinction on the North-West Frontier of India and Afghanistan in 1863-4 and became greatly experienced in all the requisites for equipping an army on active service.

Commanding 1st Division, Lieutenant-General G. H. S. Willis, CB, was born in 1822. He served with the 77th (East Middlesex) Regiment during the early phase of the Crimean War. Holding numerous senior appointments, he was Assistant Quarter-master-General of 4th Division and served in Gibraltar,

British Commanders	
General Commanding-in-Chief	Lieutenant-General Sir Garnet Wolseley, GCB, GCMG
Chief of Staff	Lieutenant-General Sir John Adye, KCB
Cavalry Division	Major-General D.C. Drury Lowe, CB
I Cavalry Brigade	Brigadier-General Sir Baker C. Russell, KCMG, CB
2 Cavalry Brigade	Brigadier-General H.C. Wilkinson, HP
Ist Infantry Division	Lieutenant-General G.H.S. Willis, CB
I Infantry Brigade	Major-General HRH the Duke of Connaught, KG, KT, GCSI, GCMG
2 Infantry Brigade	Major-General Gerald Graham, VC, CB, RE
2nd Infantry Division	Lieutenant-General Sir Edward Hamley, KCMG, CB, RA
Ist Infantry Brigade	Major-General Sir Archibald Alison, KCB
2nd Infantry Brigade	Major-General Sir Evelyn Wood, VC, GCMG, KCB
India Contingent	Major-General Sir Herbert Macpherson, VC, KCB, BSc
Mediterranean Fleet	Vice-Admiral Sir Frederick Beauchamp Paget Seymour, GCB
East India Station	Rear-Admiral Sir William Hewitt, VC, KCB

Malta and Southern District. In 1878 he was appointed Major-General Commanding Northern district, and was promoted to lieutenant-general in 1880.

Lieutenant-General Sir Edward Hamley, KCMG, CB, RA, commanding 2nd Division, saw action in most of the major Crimean War battles. He was the author of the definitive work, *The Operations of War*.

Commanding the Guards Brigade in 1st Division in Egypt, was Major-General His Royal Highness Arthur, Duke of Connaught, KG, KT, GCSI, GCMG. Born in 1850, he was a lieutenant in the Royal Enginers in 1868, a lieutenant in the Royal Artillery in 1869 and held the same rank in the Rifle Brigade during that year. After numerous appointments as brigade-major, in 1880 he was appointed General of Brigade at Aldershot. He had not seen active service before coming to Egypt.

In command of 2 Brigade was Major-General George Graham, CB, VC, RE. He joined the Royal Engineers in 1850 and had risen to his present rank by 1881. He was awarded the Victoria Cross for his conduct at the storming of the Redan at Sevastopol during the Crimean War, where he was twice wounded. He was also wounded during the China War of 1860 when he took part in the storming of the Taku Forts. Wolseley was to choose him as a divisional commander for the Sudan Campaign of 1884, in which he fought with his customary bravery and energy.

Commanding 3 Brigade was Major-General Sir Archibald Alison, KCB. Born in 1826, he joined the 72nd (Duke of Albany's Own Highlanders) Regiment of Foot 1853. He served in the Crimean War, and lost an arm at the Relief of Lucknow during the Indian Mutiny; he was Wolseley's second-in-command during the Ashanti War.

Major-General Sir Evelyn Wood, GCMG, KCB, VC, commanded 4 Brigade. Born in 1838, he entered the Royal Navy in 1852 and served during the Crimean War. In 1855 he was commissioned into the army and was awarded the VC for his bravery during the Indian Mutiny. He was with Wolseley during the Ashanti War, where he organized Wood's Regiment of Natives. He served in the Kaffir Wars in South Africa in 1879, and throughout the Zulu War commanded a column in General Newdigate's division. He was again sent to South Africa in 1881 when the Transvaal War broke out and, on the death of Sir George Pomeroy Colley, took command of British troops in Natal and the Transvaal. Wood took 2nd Division to Egypt in 1883 and subsequently became Commander-in-Chief of an Egyptian army that he had personally raised. He was appointed Adjutant-General to the British Army in 1897 and was promoted to field marshal in 1903. Evelyn Wood was not a brilliant or gifted commander, but he was a sound leader of men; his dash and fearlessness caused him to shine in his many colonial wars.

Major-General William Earle, CSI, was in charge of the lines of communication. He had entered the army in 1851 and had risen to the rank of general by 1880. He served with distinction in the 44th (East Essex) Regiment during every major battle of the Crimean War. In command of the River Column in Wolseley's Sudan Expedition, he was killed at the Battle of Kirbekan in February 1885.

Major-General D. C. Drury Lowe, CB, commanded the Cavalry Brigade in Egypt. Having joined the army in 1854, he served with the 17th Lancers in the Crimea and during the Indian Mutiny. Commanding 17th Lancers in the Zulu War of 1879, he led their charge at Ulundi.

Commanding the Royal Artillery in Egypt was Brigadier-General W. H. Goodenough. He had joined the army in 1849 and served during the Indian Mutiny when he was severely wounded.

The Royal Engineers in Egypt were commanded by Brigadier-General C. B. P. N. H. Nugent, CB, who had joined the Regiment in 1845. He served in the Crimean War.

Surgeon-General James Arthur Hanbury, CB, was principal medical officer in Egypt, being specially selected for that role. He served with distinction during the Afghan War of 1878-80 and was medical officer to General Roberts's force during its famous march from Kabul to Kandahar.

Colonel the Hon. J.C. Dormer, born in 1824, served in the Crimea and was aide-de-camp to Lord

◄ The British commanders. From left to right, top to bottom, they are: Wolseley, Adye, Willis, Hamley, Wood, Alison,

HRH the Duke of Connaught, Graham, Goodenough, Earle, Dormer and Hanbury.

▲ *Vice-Admiral Sir Frederick Beauchamp Paget Seymour, commander of the British Squadron which bombarded the forts at Alexandria on 11 July 1882. Born in 1821,* *he served in the Burmese War of 1852 and led a storming-party at the capture of Pegu; He saw service in the Crimea and in New Zealand.*

Clyde during the Indian Mutiny. He was Assistant-Adjutant General to Wolseley's force in Egypt.

Major-General Sir Herbert Macpherson, KCB, BSc, VC, was in command of the India Contingent. He had seen service in the Crimean War as Adjutant of the 78th Highlanders. He served in the Persian Campaign of 1856, and was awarded the Victoria Cross while with the Highlanders at Lucknow during the Indian Mutiny. He commanded an infantry brigade in Roberts's force during the Afghan War, and was in the Bengal Staff Corps when chosen to bring the India Contingent to Egypt, where he arrived with his Staff at Suez on 21 August.

The Royal Navy also played a part in Egypt, from the very beginning when the British fleet anchored off Alexandria on 20 May 1882, under the command of Vice-Admiral Sir Frederick Beau-

champ Paget Seymour, GCB. Born in 1821, he joined the navy in 1833. He saw action in the Second Burma War of 1852-3 when he led the Fusiliers at the storming and capture of the Pegu Pagoda. He commanded the Channel Fleet 1873-7 and in 1879 was appointed Flag Officer, Mediterranean Fleet which bombarded the forts at Alexandria on 11 July 1882.

Rear-Admiral Sir William Hewitt, KCB, VC, Commander-in-Chief East India Station, commanded a squadron that took a more than useful part in the operations; later he took possession of Suez. He went on to play a major role at Suakim during the Sudan War of 1884-5.

The Egyptian Commanders

Arabi Pasha, leader of the Egyptian Nationalist Party and commander of their forces during the War of 1882 was born in 1836, in the Province of Sharkiyeh in Lower Egypt. His full name was Saiad Ahmad Bey Arabi, and he claimed descent in the male line from Husseyn, the youngest grandson of the Prophet Mahomed, which qualified him to be considered of a family reputed holy by Muslims, although his mother was an Egyptian, and an 'Arab of the Arabs'. These facts account for the respect given him by his fellow-soldiers.

While still a boy, he had joined the Egyptian Army as a private soldier, but being of superior mind and education, rose rapidly to the rank of lieutenant-colonel in the days of Said Pasha. During the reign of Ismail he was accused of a crime, but it was a false charge and amply disproved; nevertheless, Ismail cashiered him, and this served to reinforce in Arabi the realization of the injustice afflicting his native land, and made him a determined enemy of the Turks, and of all despotic power. In 1873 he was reinstated and, perceived as a martyr, he became the most popular man in the army. In the spring of 1881, having taken a prominent part in an army remonstration against pay arrears, he was arrested but released after an outcry and, recognizing that the country accepted him as champion of popular rights, led the Cairo garrison to the Abdin Palace. Conceding to his demands, the Government made him a Pasha and appointed him Secretary for War, which made him one of the most important men in the country. But not even his staunchest adherent could have foreseen that within the space of a few months he would venture to defy the whole of Europe, and carry on his disruptive activities under the very guns of a hostile fleet that had been sent to overawe him.

Mahmoud Fehmy, said to be Arabi's second-in-command, was captured at Kassassin, before the battle, when straying into the British area of operations. The status of Ali Rubi Pasha, com-mander at Tel el-Kebir, can be gauged from the fact that he was said to 'sleep in Arabi's tent'. Alleged 'right-hand man' Mahmoud Sami Pasha, was of Turkish origin; and another prominent officer at Tel el-Kebir was Raschid Bey. At Damietta, Abdullah Pasha commanded 6,000 Negro troops; and Toulba Pasha, said to be a 'truculent lieutenant' to Arabi, commanded at Kafr ed-Dauar. Other named leaders include Yacoub Pasha Samy; Ali Fehmi; and the Bedouin chief Abou Hassam.

▶ *Arabi Pasha, aged 46, commander of the opposing Egyptian Army. He was appointed Secretary for War by the Khedive (who also made him a Pasha) after leading the Cairo garrison of the Abdin Palace in 1881 in a remonstration about arrears of pay.*

THE OPPOSING ARMIES

Sergeant of the 1st Battalion, the Black Watch. The helmet, regimental hackle and 'valise' equipment have all been stained with tea. (Pierre Turner)

The British Army in Egypt

There is some confusion as to the uniforms worn by British troops in Egypt in 1882. The campaign is confirmed as being the only one in which some British soldiers wore a grey uniform on active service, serge tunics of that colour being issued in Egypt in September 1882. (30,000 suits of this grey serge clothing had been sent out there.) Grey serge frock-coats and trousers had been sealed as patterns for this campaign. The only British troops to be clad entirely in khaki (with the exception of those of the India Contingent) were the 1st Battalion Royal Irish Fusiliers – a commentator mentioning, 'the Royal Irish, conspicuous in their hideous khaki (or kharkee) coloured uniforms'. It was said that they aroused unfavourable comment when landing at Plymouth, thus dressed, in September 1885.

Before the issue of the grey tunics, British infantry must have worn their usual scarlet field service tunic, some with cuff facings. *Army Regulations 1881* had simplified the facing colours of the British line infantry into blue for Royal regiments; yellow for Highland regiments; white for British line; and green for Irish regiments. But it is doubtful whether many units had actually changed their old facing colours before leaving for Egypt; for example, it is known the Berkshire Regiment wore their traditional light-green instead of the new white facings.

British line infantry ex Home and Mediterranean stations wore the white Wolseley helmet, with pagris, without a spike and with a brass chin-chain. The Highland Light Infantry wore a khaki helmet, otherwise units wore Home Service headdress. British cavalry were dressed as for Home Service, with some regiments wearing blue puttees in lieu of riding-boots; they wore a white helmet with no spike, pagris and chin-chains; it is likely that most pagris were white, although the Household Cavalry are often shown with a crimson

▶ *A 'fashion plate' showing the dress of the Guards in Egypt 1882. These officers and men of the 1st Life Guards and the Grenadier Guards, fresh out from England, are equipped for foreign service.*

pagri, and the 19th Hussars with dark-blue. No cavalry unit seems to have worn a dyed helmet at Tel el-Kebir; but local dyeing of helmets, belts and pouches with brown colouring material, tobacco-juice or tea was carried out. The cavalry were issued with blue-glass goggles and green veils, carbine-slings and fly-fringing for the horses' eyes.

Mounted Infantry wore their own regimental dress, with a white helmet – some bearing a regimental plate; twill trousers or breeches were worn with high canvas or leather gaiters; no spurs; normal infantry equipment and brown leather cartridge bandolier over the left shoulder; the Martini-Henry rifle with bayonet was carried; sergeants carried a steel three-bar hilted cavalry sword in a steel scabbard suspended from the waist-belt by a brown leather sling.

The Royal Horse Artillery gunners wore blue stable jackets with red braided collars and plain cuffs; blue riding-breeches with red stripes, and riding-boots with buckled-on spurs; white helmet with a white pagri, chin-chain and spike ornaments; white pouch belts and waist-belts, a pistol in a white case on left hip, white pouches on right hip. Officers' helmets bore a ball ornament. Royal Field Artillery wore much the same; in both branches some officers and men wore breeches of a pinkish-khaki colour.

Royal Marine Light Infantry wore a scarlet serge frock-coat with blue collar, cuffs and shoulder-straps; blue trousers with red stripe (later, in Cairo on a ceremonial parade, they wore white duck trousers), white helmet with white pagris; white equipment with crossbelts (which was probably dyed later).

The Early Wearing of Khaki

Both the British and Indian infantry units of the India Contingent wore khaki, although it was not adopted officially as a universal uniform (in both drill and serge) until May 1885. Other ranks wore a khaki sun-helmet, officers a spiked helmet. The Seaforth Highlanders of the contingent wore khaki doublet, regimental trews, with canvas gaiters coming high up the thigh (officers wore tartan puttees). A large cartridge-box on a shoulder-belt, bayonet on a waist-belt, and a slanting row of seven loops on each breast for rifle cartridges, was standard for other ranks. Indian infantry wore a khaki uniform with cartridge-loops, khaki puttees, coloured breeches, and were armed with Snider rifles. Indian cavalry wore their habitual uniform, with blue puttees.

The Naval Brigade

At Alexandria, the Naval Brigade wore a blue jumper and trousers, white gaiters, and a blue cap; a modified valise equipment with pouches on a waist-belt, and shoulder-braces. There were variations, some had white cap covers, others wore the braid Sennet hat with a white jumper, blue collar, black silk, and blue bell-bottomed trousers. An existing photograph shows a 9pdr gun detachment in blue jumpers, white vests and black silks, and white trousers with high canvas gaiters and ankle-boots. Their equipment was brown leather naval pattern;

◀ *Seamen of the landing-party sent ashore on 13 July to police the streets of Alexandria, under command of Lord Charles Beresford, RN, fire on the mob with a Gatling gun.*

Martini-Henry rifle, with a large cutlass-bayonet carried in a frog on the left. Some sailors carried a revolver with white lanyard attached, in various waist-belt positions. Some sailors and petty officers had a white rolled blanket slung over the shoulder.

Naval officers wore a blue reefer jacket, blue trousers and a white cap-cover; some wore a dyed or khaki helmet with a white pagri; a single-breasted five-button frock-coat with a low standing collar; rank shown in usual manner on the sleeve. A high, stiff white shirt collar was visible beneath the coat collar, which was sometimes turned down to reveal collar and tie. In most cases white trousers were worn, with high leather boots, or canvas gaiters and ankle-boots like the ratings. The naval pattern officers' sword was carried in a frog on the left of a form of Sam Browne belt with a single brace; officers had a pistol holster and cartridge-pouches on the belt; and a white lanyard. Officers' uniform was not issue at this date and they seem to have enjoyed a certain amount of leeway in the matter of dress. Many officers landed at Alexandria lacking a service, or indeed any uniform at all, and a variety of exotic dress could be seen (one Guards officer arrived with a morning-coat and top-hat) and had to be outfitted from scratch.

The Equipment of the British Soldier

The 'valise' pattern equipment was worn, but in Egypt the valise itself was not carried. Generally introduced into the Army in 1871, valise-pattern equipment replaced the old knapsack with a black waterproof canvas bag (the valise) worn at the small of the back and supported over the shoulders by straps split into three at the level of the third button of the tunic. These straps fastened to a waist-belt holding two pouches, one on each side of the belt-clasp, each containing 20 rounds of ammunition with a further 30 rounds carried in a 'ball bag' slung below the right-hand pouch. When full, these pouches partially balanced the valise, which had the rolled cape and the mess-tin level with the wearer's neck. The bayonet, longer than previously, was carried on the left side of the waist-belt with the haversack, its position causing it to catch between the man's legs when he was running. When firing from the prone position, ammunition tended to fall out of the pouches; this was a major flaw because the introduction of the rapid breech-loading rifle meant that much firing was carried out in this position. When firing from behind low cover the right elbow was exposed as the arm was raised to extract a round from the right-hand pouch. Hurriedly rising to his feet to advance at the double, the soldier had to fasten the pouch, grab his bayonet to keep it clear of his legs, and steady his head-dress to stop it falling off – at the same time he had to carry his rifle.

Weapons

The personal weapon carried by all infantry in the Egyptian Campaign was the Martini-Henry Mark III of 1879 which, with its smaller bore, greater range, lower trajectory and superior accuracy, allied to easy operation and quick reloading, was far in advance of any hand-weapon previously issued to the British soldier. The simplicity and efficiency of the Martini-Henry justified claims that it was one of the best smallarms ever designed, yet it suffered from serious defects. It was liable to jam if sand got into the mechanism, which happened repeatedly throughout the campaign; and fouling lodged readily in the deep and square-cut grooves of its rifling. Also the kick of the recoil was vicious, especially if the bore were foul; shoulders were bruised after a few rounds and nose bleed was not uncommon; and, despite the protection of a wooden forestock, prolonged firing soon made the barrel too hot to touch. Its bore was .450 inches; it fired a black-powder .45 calibre centre-fire, Boxer cartridge of thin rolled brass, with a heavy lead slug weighing 480 grains, paper-wrapped at its base to prevent melting in its passage down the bore. The breech-block was hinged at the rear and dropped to expose the chamber when the lever behind the trigger-guard was depressed to flip out the expended case. A fresh round was laid on top of the grooved block and thumbed home, and the lever was raised to cock the rifle. There was no safety-catch. The rifle was sighted for firing at 500 yards' range at which distance the trajectory was 8.1 feet, far less than in any previous British rifle. Weighing 9 pounds, it was 71½ inches long, 49½ inches without the bayonet.

In trained hands the rifle was accurate to 1,000 yards and more; battalion volley-fire against massed targets frequently opened at 600–800 yards, and even an average marksman could score hits at 300–400 yards. The soft-lead slug was a man-stopper that smashed bone and cartilage, leaving wicked wounds, and the enemy were usually literally 'blown-away' by sheer fire-power – as was the fate of innumerable Afghans, Afridis, Dervishes, Egyptians, Zulus and a host of other native tribesmen in various Victorian colonial wars. But the Martini-Henry was a single-shot weapon and its life was inevitably short, because of the demand for magazine repeating rifles – among the last occasions when it was used in battle was by Kitchener's Sudanese battalions and the Egyptian Army during the Omdurman campaign of 1896.

The bayonet, 21½ inches long, was frequently reported to be found wanting in action and there seems little doubt that it was not much good. Mostly imported and case-hardened, subsequent regrinding or even deep polishing removed the hardened shell to leave a blade that could be easily bent or twisted.

The British cavalry sword was similarly castigated. It was 35 inches long, slightly curved to improve the cutting edge, and had a bowl-shell hand-guard. The Egyptian Campaign brought the sword's failings to light, its users bitterly complaining that the weapon was too straight and too blunt, so that the enemy had to be put out with the point.

In 1880 the Enfield Small Arms factory designed and produced for military use a revolver which, although not particularly good, became the official pattern for both Army and Navy. It was the first revolver to be on general issue to cavalry rank-and-file. The Mark I Pattern of 1880 had a calibre of .422 inches, which was eventually considered to have insufficient weight to stop a charging man at short range.

The Gatling Gun

The Naval Machine-Gun Battery employed during the campaign was formed at Ismaila. It numbered fifteen officers and 197 seamen serving six Gatling guns, giving each gun a crew of two officers and eighteen men. To replace casualties and guard the guns on the march, a company of three officers and about 45 files escorted the battery.

Coming into British service in 1871 as the first effective machine-gun, the Gatling had ten .45-inch breech-loading rifle barrels grouped together; a cartridge feed-case fitted into a magazine-hopper, the cartridges dropping by gravity into the breeches of

Lieutenant Colonel of the 2nd Life Guards. He wears an anti-fly net around his helmet. Normally he would carry a pistol on the 'Sam Browne' belt. (Pierre Turner)

▲ A Gatling gun in an emplacement at Port Said, two or three days after the British occupied the town and removed the Egyptian garrison. A small earthwork to pro- *tect the town from attack by enemy troops lurking a few miles distant was thrown up by sailors and marines and named by them Fort Royal.*

the barrels, revolved by a crank-handle, each successively firing once per revolution. It fired heavy bullets at more than 600 rounds a minute, a high and terrifying concentration of fire that made it an ideal weapon for colonial campaigns of the period. Initially manned by sailors, Gatling guns on mobile carriages were taken ashore by naval landing-parties complete with limber, shafts and harness. By 1875 they had been issued to the Royal Artillery who were trained to handle them as field-guns. Newbolt's poem told of the Gatling that jammed, a common fault caused by the base of ordinary service rifle cartridges being torn off by the gun's extractor, leaving the metal case jammed tight in the chamber; it was obviated by specially made solid-drawn cartridge cases of the American type.

At the naval bombardment of the land forts at Alexandria, which prefaced the land campaign, it was claimed that Gatling guns firing from the ships' foretops played an important part in the success of the operation. Certainly in his report of the action Admiral Seymour stated that the demoralization of the Egyptian gunners was mainly due to the hail of bullets poured into them at close-range from the foretop of the little *Condor*, but it seems that the Gatling received credit due elsewhere!

It is known that Lord Charles Beresford, commanding *Condor*, asked Admiral Seymour for permission to borrow and mount a machine-gun in his foretop. Subsequently a Nordenfelt was sent to the maintop and kept up a rapid fire throughout the bombardment, firing 30–40,000 rounds at close range down into the embrasures, which greatly demoralized the Egyptian gunners. In 1917, however, A. Hilliard Atteridge and F .V. Longstaff in their *Book of the Machine Gun* (Hugh Rees, London 1917) decry the value of these guns employed in such a fashion: 'At the bombardment of Alexandria in the summer of 1882 machine guns were mounted in the tops of ships, in order to bring a plunging fire upon Egyptian batteries, but the results were disappointing, probably on account of smoke obscuring the view; the ranging was bad, and an examination of the batteries after the bombardment showed very few marks of machine-gun bullets. During the attack the gunners in the tops of the ships were wrapped in a fog of powder-smoke from the big guns lower down, and the machine guns themselves produced another dense cloud round the tops. One may say that smokeless powder is almost a necessity for the thoroughly efficient working of any kind of quick-firing gun, whether cannon or machine gun.'

Nevertheless, Gatling guns came into their own three days later when a party of bluejackets and marines landed at Alexandria, the effective use of their guns being recounted by Lord Charles Beresford, as reported in *The Army and Navy Gazette* of 4 November 1882:

'When the Gatling guns were landed at Alexandria, after the bombardment, the effect of their fire upon the wild mob of fanatic incendiaries and looters was quite extraordinary. These guns were not fired at the people, but a little over their heads, as a massacre would have been the result had the guns been steadily trained on the mob. The rain of bullets, which they heard screaming over their heads, produced a moral effect not easily described. I asked an Egyptian officer, some weeks afterwards, how on earth it was that Arabi and his 9,000 regular

◀ *One of the 40pdr guns brought into position against the Egyptians south of Ramleh. The British presence at Ramleh, east of Alexandria, kept Arabi's forces occupied while the main British force went to Ismailia so as to come into the theatre of operations from a completely different direction. The Egyptians were strongly positioned, and numerous pieces were brought into position facing them.*

troops, who were within five miles, did not march down upon the town in the first four days after the bombardment, when Arabi knew that Captain Fisher's Naval Brigade, which held the lines, numbered less than 400 men. The Egyptian officer replied, "That he knew no army which could face machines which 'pumped lead', and that all the gates were defended by such machines, as well as having torpedoes under the bridges, such defences could not be faced." This certainly was the case. I believe the Egyptian officer spoke the truth, and that the moral effect produced by the Gatling on the people in the first landing prevented the army from attacking the diminutive force which held the lines afterwards.

'Replying for "The Navy", at a dinner of the Cutler's Company, Lord Charles Beresford said: "The great value of machine guns has been shown. With the Gatlings, the landing parties had cleared the streets of Alexandria and prevented Arabi from returning, and, if they had been allowed to land immediately after the bombardment, they might have dispersed the crowds laden with loot, have captured Arabi, Toalba Pasha, and other leaders, and saved the town; but the Government had promised that no man should land, and they were bound by the promise." 'In my opinion, machine guns, if properly worked, would decide the fate of a campaign, and would be equally useful ashore or afloat.'

The Army and Navy Gazette of 14 October 1882 reported the success of the Gatlings at the final battle of the campaign, at Tel el-Kebir on 12 September 1882:

'The naval machine gun battery, consisting of six Gatlings, manned by thirty seamen, reached the position assigned to it in the English lines on September 10th and, on Tuesday, September 12th, received orders to advance. They came within easy range of the Tel el-Kebir earthworks, and observed guns in front, guns to the right, guns to the left, and a living line of fire above them. Nothing daunted, the order, "action-front" was given, and was taken up joyously by every gun's crew. Round whisked the Gatlings, r-r-r-r-r-rum! r-r-r-r-r-rum! r-r-r-r-r-rum! that hellish noise the soldier so much detests in action, not for what it has done, so much as what it could do, rattled out. The report of the machine guns, as they rattle away, rings out clearly on the

morning air. The parapets are swept. The embrasures are literally plugged with bullets. The flashes cease to come from them. With a cheer the bluejackets double over the dam, and dash over the parapet, only just in time to find their enemy in full retreat. That machine gun was too much for them. Skulking under the parapet were found a few poor devils, too frightened to retire, yet willing enough to stab a Christian, if helpless and wounded. The trenches were full of dead. But few wounded were found. Captain Fitz Roy led his men most gallantly, and followed up the retreating foe until the main camp was reached. Here the halt was sounded. Admiral Sir Beauchamp Seymour and staff now came up and addressed the battery, complimenting the officers and men on their gallantry.'

The Artillery

In Egypt in 1882, the Royal Artillery guns were all rifled, muzzle-loading pieces (RML), distributed as follows:

The Field Artillery was equipped with 13pdrs and 16pdrs; Horse Artillery with either 9pdrs or 13pdrs; Siege Train with 25pdrs and 40pdrs, and 6.3in howitzers; Mountain Artillery with the 7pdr 'screw-gun'.

At the Battle of Tel el-Kebir, Batteries A/1, D/1, I/2 and N/2 all had 16pdrs. C/3 and J/3 Batteries had 13pdrs; H/1 had 9pdrs. 'C' Battery of 3 Brigade had long-trail 13pdr guns, with carriages, and special patent ammunition wagons which carried their projectiles vertically in top-lid boxes.

The 9pdr and 16pdr rifled muzzle-loading guns were considered to be inferior to foreign artillery, and in 1878 they were replaced by a 13pdr rifled muzzle-loading gun fitted with axle-tree seats for both Horse and Field Artillery. In design, this gun represented a great advance, the use of slow-burning powder allowing longer barrels; but the excessive recoil of the 13pdr caused it to be unpopular with its users.

Also introduced was the 2.5in rifled, muzzle-loading gun for Mountain Artillery – this was the famous 'screw-gun' whose barrel was in two parts which screwed together. Designed in 1880 by Colonel C.B. le Mesurier, RA, and made of steel, it was a rifled, muzzle-loading, jointed 7pdr gun weighing 400 pounds, its increased length and weight due to the muzzle and breech being in two portions, screwed together by a trunnion hoop. Broken-down into separate pieces, each making a single load for a mule, this grand little gun was transported over mountain paths and passes denied to the ordinary field-gun. It threw its 7lb projectile most effectively in many campaigns.

Fellah, *Egyptian Army, 1882. A large pack was worn on the back with blankets and rolled greatcoat. The rifle is the Remington rolling-block pattern with brass-hilted sword bayonet.* (Michael Roffe)

Each battery comprised six guns and carriages, with limbers and ammunition-wagons; one ammunition/store wagon; one store-limber wagon; one forge-wagon; one water-cart; and one cavalry spring-cart.

Each Horse Artillery battery and the 13pdr batteries of the Field Artillery carried 180 rounds of common shell; 648 shrapnel rounds; 24 caseshot; reserve ammunition of 2,000 common; 720 shrapnel and 28 rounds of case, giving a total of 300 rounds per gun.

Each 16pdr battery carried 144 common, 432 shrapnel and 24 rounds of caseshot; with 288 common; 864 shrapnel and 48 case in reserve, giving 300 rounds per gun.

In addition, each battery carried 800 incendiary star-shells of suitable calibre for both 13pdr and 16pdr guns.

The Siege Train had 200 rounds for each gun, plus 100 of the new pattern star-shells for the howitzers. Two Nolan range-finders and ten new-pattern clinometers were also provided.

The number of rounds expended during the campaign was thus: 280 at Magfar on 24 August; 250 at Mahsama on 25 August; 154 at Kassassin on 29 August; 278 at Kassassin on 9 September; 75 at Tel el-Kebir on 13 September; a total expenditure of 1,437 rounds.

The Egyptian Army in 1882

During the 19th century the Egyptian Army had had a checkered career; its defeat by the Ethiopians in the late 1870s had reduced it to a bad state by the early 1880s. The best troops seem to have been the Sudanese battalions raised from the Africans of the south; the best native Egyptian battalions were stationed in Egypt, those sent to the Sudan usually went as a punishment. At this time a battalion consisted of four companies (*buluks*) each approximately 200 strong.

The Egyptian military system was adapted to secure maximum strength in wartime, or minimum when the army was on a peacetime footing; every soldier passing through the ranks could be recalled, and a large portion of the male population could be mustered if needed. Villages were raided to provide levies of fresh men who received arms and ammuni-

▲ *Arabi Pasha leads his troops to war through the streets of Alexandria, July 1882. Mostly conscripts and usually unwilling recruits, the Egyptian soldiers nevertheless put on a creditable show at the bombardment of Alexandria and, although quickly defeated, showed up well on occasions at Kassassin and Tel el-Kebir.*

▶ *Recruiting for the Egyptian Army: a detachment of forcibly enlisted recruits on their way to garrisons at Cairo or Alexandria. Extremely averse to military service, recruits were often manacled like felons.*

tion, but no uniform and little training. Whole companies were summarily drafted from one battalion to another if suspected of disloyalty. At the time of the Arabi Pasha rebellion the army was weaker than at any period in its history, its strength being only six regiments of infantry (9,000 men); two regiments of cavalry (1,000); one regiment of field artillery (600); one regiment of coastal artillery (700) totalling in all only 11,300 men, but all being old soldiers. Large numbers of veterans must have been recalled to the Colours and numerous *fellahin* (Egyptian peasants) dragged from their homes and

◀ *A parade of Egyptian troops in Cairo at the time of the War of 1882.*

▼ *Egyptian infantry in camp, part of an army composed of different races and ethnic groups such as Arabs of various tribes, Negroes from the Sudan, and Bedouin tribesmen; but a high proportion were ordinary peasants (*fellahin*) forcibly conscripted by Arabi – this group may well be such troops.*

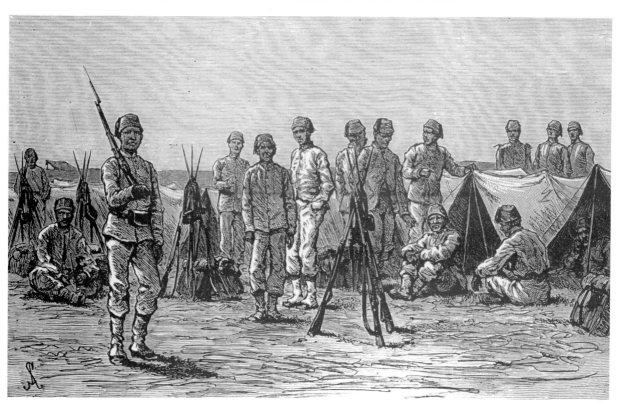

formed into regiments that could have had little cohesion or confidence in one another.

Arabi Pasha had about 60,000 fighting men disposed at the likeliest places all over the Delta – in the neighbourhood of Alexandria, at Cairo, and at Tel el-Kebir, a commanding point on the railway between Ismailia and the capital. It was an army made up of different races and ethnic groups – Negroes of the Sudan, Arabs of various tribes, and large numbers of Bedouin tribesmen; a fairly high proportion were *fellahin* conscripted by Arabi. A war-correspondent of *The Globe* wrote that, at Tel el-Maskhuta, there were many dead wearing brown felt head-coverings of peasants, besides numerous woven palm-leaf baskets used to carry provisions. Wolseley did not consider it a formidable army, but feared that Arabi might arouse Mohammedan fanaticism to a pitch that could transform the scale and scope of the struggle.

Although Arabi had a basis of well-trained men and many field guns, rifles and stores, he lacked efficient officers and NCOs, but he did have unlimited numbers of excellent workmen to build military works. The emphasis on fortification at Kafr ed-Dauar, Tel el-Kebir and other places undoubtedly arose from his common-sense disinclination to meet the British in an open and general action; it was thought that if he held out until the Nile was high enough, he could cause infinite trouble.

The Dress of the Egyptian Army

The rebel Egyptian infantry wore the small red fez (*tarboosh*) with a short black tassel hanging from its top, black tunic, and trousers of coarse white cotton cloth; the tunic had a low round-fronted standing collar, six buttons in a single row, with badges and buckles all of brass bearing the star and crescent. Loose trousers and white canvas gaiters were worn over black leather shoes; all equipment was black leather including straps on the field-pack which was brown or black and had a cooking-pot strapped to it, and a grey blanket-roll wrapped round it, or slung over the left shoulder and around the body. A brass-hilted, wavy-bladed sword-bayonet was carried on the left side in a brass-mounted steel scabbard. Officers wore a very dark-blue single-breasted short thigh-length tunic, with voluminous skirts and

a row of eight yellow metal buttons; with it was worn a white shirt and black stock. On the shoulders were gold-fringed epaulettes, varying to indicate rank. Trousers, the same colour as the tunic, were full and tapered towards the ankles. Head-dress was a red *tarboosh* with long black tassel hanging from the crown. A black leather waist-belt had a square yellow metal buckle bearing star and crescent; swords were either steel, three-bar hilted in a plain steel scabbard, or white hilted *Mameluke*-type sword in black leather with yellow metal scabbard. Cavalry were dressed in the same manner as the infantry, with black pouch-belt over left shoulder, and black waist-belt and slings carrying a steel, three-bar hilted sword in a steel scabbard. Short black boots without spurs were worn in place of gaiters.

Weapons of the Egyptian Army

Infantry were armed with the Remington 11mm (.433) rolling-block repeater rifle, capable of seventeen shots a minute; made in the USA under contract, 60,000 had been delivered by 1876. It was also supplied as a carbine for cavalry and a musketoon for artillery; the sword-bayonet was mounted on the right side of the barrel. In view of problems with sand leading to 'hanging-up' of lock and breech-mechanism, oil was never used on Remington rifles, which were so rubbed by their owners as to look as though made of silver. The Egyptians' musketry left much to be desired and was always better at long rather than at short range;

Ordnance captured at Tel el-Kebir				
Gun	Number captured	Calibre (cm)	No of Grooves	Weight of shell lb. oz.
Bronze, RML La Hitte	7	9	6	8 6
Steel, RBL Krupp, Essen, 1871	47	9	16	14 10
Steel, RBL Krupp, Essen, 1871	10	8	12	9 14

Eight of the Krupp guns listed above, with four 7pdr rifled bronze guns, were captured in their gun-pits by General Macpherson's force on the south side of the battlefield.

at Tel el-Kebir, eighteen infantry battalions, advantageously posted, poured out hails of fire, but only killed two men! Conscripts were armed with old brass-mounted, muzzle-loading muskets.

The Egyptian artillery consisted mostly of Krupp field-pieces, of the pattern used by the Prussians in their 1870 war against the French; they

Private of the General Post Office Rifles. These troops, mostly Post Office workers, provided a Telegraphic Detachment for the expeditionary force. (Michael Roffe)

were only slightly inferior to the ordinary muzzle-loading British guns. Eighty of these guns were divided equally between the lines at Kafr ed-Dauar and Tel el-Kebir, with two field batteries; *mitrailleuse* and rocket batteries were also at both places.

In addition, Arabi's army was equipped with some Gardner guns of a rare single-barrelled model chambered for the same 11mm (.433) cartridges as used in their Remington rifles; and a few Gatling guns, presumably of the same calibre.

Egyptian Dispositions

At the time of the bombardment of Alexandria, the Egyptian Army consisted of about 9,000 men; 48 batteries of six guns each, totalling 288 field-guns, but with only 750 limber-horses. In Alexandria were 5,000 of these troops, the remainder being distributed throughout the country. Ten days after the bombardment, the force at Arabi's disposal at Kafr ed-Dauar was only about 6,500 men; the Bedouin did not begin to come in until fifteen days later. At this stage, Army Reservists, some of them more than 50 years of age, were called to the Colours, raising the strength of the army to about 60,000 men.

At the time of Wolseley's seizure of Ismailia, this army was distributed as follows: 15,000 at Kafr ed-Dauar; 15,000 at Aboukir, Rosetta and Burlus; 7,000 at Damietta; 12,000 at Tel el-Kebir and on the eastern side of the Delta; 11,000 at Cairo. In addition, of the Bedouin beginning to come in, about 3,000 went to Kafr ed-Dauar, and about 3,000 to Tel el-Kebir.

As soon as the Council in Cairo learned of the taking of Ismailia, it determined greatly to enlarge the army and, by enlisting completely untrained recruits, its strength was raised to 100,000 men; after a few days' drill, these unfortunates were drafted into the ranks to take their places with the trained soldiers. There were sufficient rifles to arm them all, but initially only enough clothing and equipment for 40,000; but strenuous efforts quickly raised sufficient for the entire army. Through the 'goodwill of the people' 11,000 transport animals were procured; field-guns being horsed by the same means, although all horses were untrained.

FROM ALEXANDRIA TO TEL EL-KEBIR

Major-General Sir Archibald Alison arrived from England on 17 July 1882 to help keep order in Alexandria. His small force consisted of The King's Royal Rifle Corps; the South Staffordshire Regiment; a battalion of Royal Marine Light Infantry and a substantial number of sailors from ships in the harbour. Total strength was 3,755 men plus seven 9pdr, two 7pdr guns, six Gatlings and four rocket-tubes. Later in the campaign, General Alison commanded the Highland Brigade in General Hamley's 2nd Infantry Division.

Alison sent out reconnaissance patrols in all directions to determine the whereabouts and strength of the enemy forces; great use was made of an armoured train devised by Captain Fisher, RE and manned by sailors, which ran on railway lines that constituted the only practical road to the east. Here Arabi was subsequently found, entrenching himself in force at Kafr ed-Dauar where there were said (by prisoners) to be 12,000 men of the Regular Army and 4,000 Bedouin; it was also revealed that a force of 5,000 Regular infantry, 5,000 Bedouin, 1,000 cavalry with twelve Krupp guns were entrenching themselves on the Sweetwater canal near Ismailia.

▼ *The initial operations of 1882 took place in the area of Ramleh, where the British entrenched themselves opposite the enemy. The Egyptians sent out patrols so that there were occasional 'affairs at the outpost'. The skirmish illustrated below involved the mounted infantry.*

◄ *Top left: the British position at Ramleh, east of Alexandria. The main body having gone to Ismailia, a strong force remained to hold the position. The 40pdr guns are seen being inspected by the Duke of Connaught.*

◄ *The strip of land between Lake Aboukir and Lake Marcotis, where the railway and canal run side by side, was inter-sected by Arabi's en-trenched positions. Here British infantry and artillerymen improve their positions opposite those those of the enemy.*

▲ *The Naval Brigade skirmishing ahead of the armoured train, part of the reconnaissance-in-force of 5 August, towards Kindj Osman, the nearest point of Arabi's fortified position.*

Skirmishes and outpost engagements occurred daily as the British advanced to take Ramleh which was speedily fortified and artillery emplaced on the heights from which the Egyptian lines could clearly be seen. Sharp actions took place involving the armoured train, its guns engaging the Egyptian guns while infantry detrained and skirmished. Marines, sailors and men of the South Staffords and

Alexandria to Kafr ed-Dauar

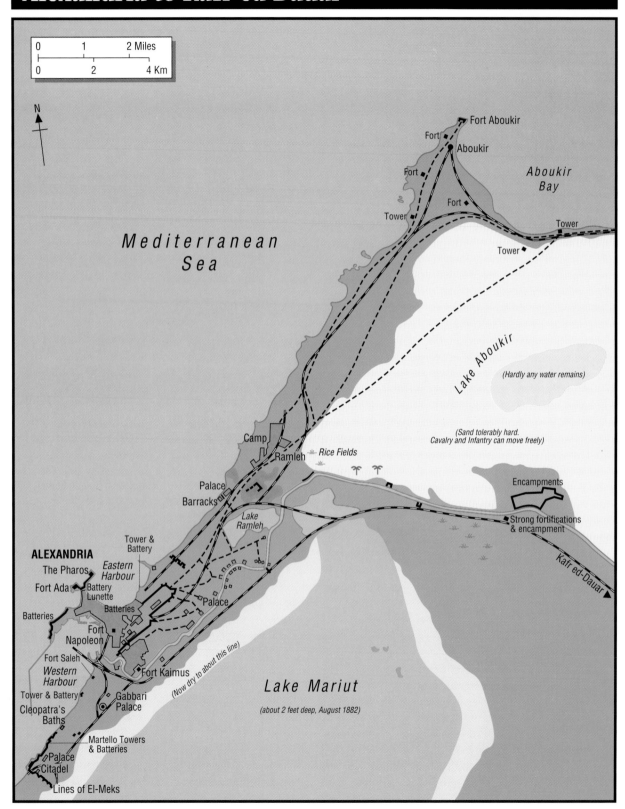

0   1   2 Miles
0   2   4 Km

N

Fort Aboukir

Fort

Aboukir

Aboukir Bay

Fort

Fort

Tower

Tower

Tower

Tower

M e d i t e r r a n e a n S e a

Lake Aboukir

(Hardly any water remains)

(Sand tolerably hard. Cavalry and Infantry can move freely)

Camp

Ramleh

Rice Fields

Encampments

Palace
Barracks

Strong fortifications & encampment

Lake Ramleh

Tower & Battery

Kafr ed-Dauar

ALEXANDRIA

The Pharos

Eastern Harbour

Fort Ada

Battery
Lunette

Batteries

Palace

Batteries

Fort
Napoleon

Fort Saleh

(Now dry to about this line)

Western Harbour

Fort Kaimus

Lake Mariut

Tower & Battery

Gabbari
Palace

(about 2 feet deep, August 1882)

Cleopatra's Baths

Martello Towers
& Batteries

Palace
Citadel

Lines of El-Meks

The naval armoured train, carrying one 40pdr and two 9pdr guns, a Nordenfelt and two Gatling machine-guns. This 'locomotive fortress' consisted of six trucks protected by iron shields, with the engine in the middle; the men in the trucks being protected by sandbags. It was manned by three companies of seamen from the naval ships in Alexandria harbour.

▲ *Wolseley's strategy involved shipping his main force to Ismailia, at the entrance to the Suez Canal, where they were landed over the course of a few days in the style shown in this sketch.*

◀ *The Guards Brigade, with the Duke of Connaught at their head, march into Ismailia.*

DCLI took part in these mini-battles against Egyptian infantry, who did not particularly distinguish themselves.

From 8 August formations of the expeditionary force began to arrive at Alexandria and by the 17th the majority were ashore. The Commander-in-Chief, Sir Garnet Wolseley, arrived on 15 August and, with his Staff and other senior officers, reconnoitred the Egyptian positions and the ground over which General Alison's men had been skirmishing and scouting since mid July.

On the 17th it was announced that the force was to embark for a landing at Aboukir Bay and move around Aboukir Lake to the rear of Arabi's position, while a frontal attack was made from Ramleh. This was a ruse and it succeeded admirably; the fleet in fact sailed past Aboukir, eastwards round the coast to Port Said, and then down the Suez Canal to Ismailia.

By the evening of 23 August, four days after leaving Alexandria, the majority of Wolseley's force were ashore at Ismailia. The essential depth of water in this stretch of the Sweetwater canal was rapidly falling and, as it was known that the Egyptians had constructed a dam across the canal at Magfar, about ten miles from Ismailia, beyond Nefisha (held by 2nd Battalion, Yorks & Lancs and some Royal Marine Artillery), Wolseley decided to send troops westwards to hold the canal as far as Magfar. These were to be commanded by General Graham, at that time at Nefisha; General Wolseley with his Staff accompanied them.

Orders issued on 23 August detailed the move:

'The following movements will take place: the three squadrons of Household Cavalry, two guns of 'M' Battery, 'A' Brigade, Royal Horse Artillery, the detachment of the 19th Hussars, and the Mounted Infantry, will march independently tomorrow morning at 4 a.m. for Nefisha, and will place themselves under the orders of Major-General Graham.

'As soon as Major-General Graham has been joined by the above troops he will proceed, together with those now under his command, to Magfar, and take up a position there. The Duke of Cornwall's Light Infantry will also proceed at the same time to Nefisha, and on arrival will remain there and protect the station, the bridge and the canal, their camp equipage being sent by rail.'

The Advance to Magfar

Following the line of the railway, the British column advanced until they neared Ramses, eight miles from Ismailia; enemy could be seen in the sandhills around the station, and their guns, emplaced in batteries, opened fire upon the column. Advancing in skirmish order, the infantry took possession of the dam across the canal between the villages of Magfar and Tel el-Maskhuta; here the Marines and the Yorks & Lancs threw up shelter-trenches under artillery fire. The British guns were positioned on a mound and the Household Cavalry, after driving-in enemy skirmishers, drew up behind sandhills, ready to charge should the enemy attack. General Wolseley immediately sent back to Nefisha for the Duke of Cornwall's Light Infantry, and to Ismailia for the Brigade of Guards and an artillery battery.

Throughout the day an uneven cannonade was kept up between the opposing forces; the enemy constantly being reinforced from Tel el-Kebir, trains bearing troops arriving in rapid succession; and two Egyptian cavalry regiments on one occasion swept round upon the British right flank, but not near enough to be charged by the Household Cavalry. Under fire from six enemy guns, the two RHA guns kept up an accurate fire which deterred an Egyptian advance; the enemy's return fire, although from well-served guns, did little damage because their percussion-fuzed shells sank deeply into the sand before exploding, while those with time-fuzes exploded high in the air. At about midday two Gatlings manned by sailors from *Orion* and a Nordenfelt from a steam-launch coming up the canal reinforced the force, and played a useful part from shelter-pits, particularly with the Yorks & Lancs on the left flank, between the canal and the railway. An enemy encircling threat on the British right, including six guns, took in part-reverse the main position held by infantry and the two guns; at about 1 p.m the DCLI marched in from Nefisha and took up position in reserve.

The heat was intense and there was little water; the Brigade of Guards, marching from Ismailia in the hottest part of the day, had many men fall by the wayside before arriving at 6.20 p.m. when the sun had set and the action petered-out. With them came the four remaining guns of N/A RHA and some

Ismailia to Kassassin

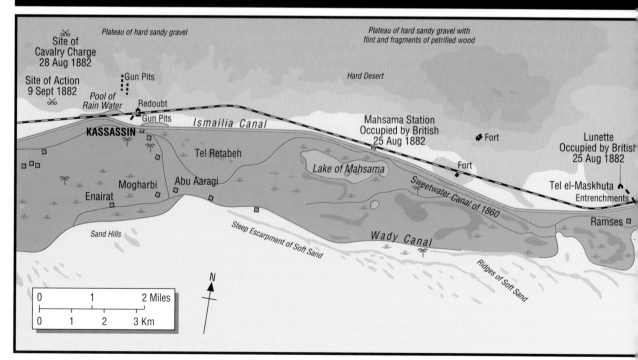

Plateau of hard sandy gravel

Plateau of hard sandy gravel with flint and fragments of petrified wood

Site of
Cavalry Charge
28 Aug 1882

Site of Action
9 Sept 1882

Hard Desert

Gun Pits

Pool of
Rain Water

Redoubt

Gun Pits

Ismailia Canal

Mahsama Station
Occupied by British
25 Aug 1882

Fort

Lunette
Occupied by British
25 Aug 1882

KASSASSIN

Tel Retabeh

Lake of Mahsama

Fort

Tel el-Maskhuta

Mogharbi

Abu Aaragi

Sweetwater Canal of 1860

Entrenchments

Enairat

Ramses

Sand Hills

Steep Escarpment of Soft Sand

Wady Canal

Ridges of Soft Sand

0   1   2 Miles
0   1   2   3 Km

N

Marine artillery; earlier Sir Baker Russell had come in with the 4th and 7th Dragoon Guards, and after midnight, A/1 Battery (16pdrs) joined the force and, at dawn, relieved the four guns of N/A on the sandhill.

Throughout the long day, the force had been under command of General Willis, who, accompanied by his Staff, had come forward with General Wolseley. The Duke of Connaught was in command of the Brigade of Guards.

Next morning General Graham's force, plus newly arrived troops, advanced against the Egyptian position at Magfar, but soon discovered that the enemy had disappeared, withdrawing their twelve guns from the positions occupied on the previous day. At this, General Wolseley sent orders to the cavalry and horse artillery to push on at once, 'to work well round the enemy's left and cut off his retreat, if possible'. But the cavalry horses were scarcely fit for such severe exertion after so recently landing from shipboard; they were not as accustomed to the terrain and conditions as the small, well-bred Egyptian horses on which the infantry were mounted.

Nevertheless, they manoeuvred as far as possible in accordance with the order until coming upon a substantial enemy force on the heights over Mahsama, where General Drury Lowe found himself opposed by a large force of infantry, with guns in position, backed by eight or ten squadrons of cavalry. The battery between the Guards and the South Staffordshire Regiment, reinforced by two guns from A/I, began to fire very effectively with shrapnel, and the enemy, also plagued by fire from the Mounted Infantry (employed in their proper function of galloping close, dismounting and then pouring well-aimed close-range fire into the enemy) began to fall back. Menaced by British cavalry bearing down towards the canal, threatening lines of retreat, the Egyptian guns limbered-up, while the Egyptian infantry were hastily entrained and carried away towards Tel el-Kebir.

◀ *On 24 August General Graham's force attacked a dam across the Sweetwater Canal at Maskhuta. This illustration shows the incident when the very first shell fired by enemy artillery burst among the General's staff, but without causing casualties.*

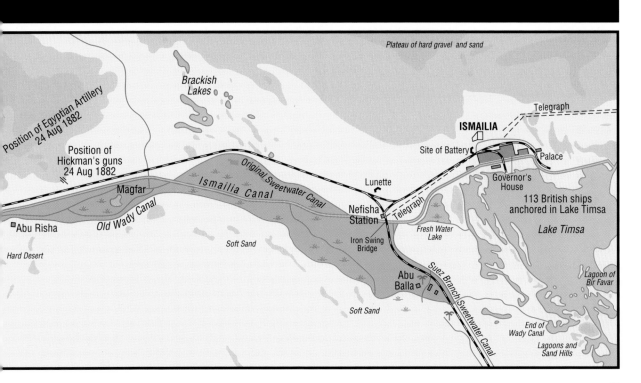

With the Mounted Infantry joining in a final cavalry charge, the camp at Mahsama was quickly captured, yielding a haul of seven Krupp guns, stores, camp equipment, large numbers of Remington rifles and plentiful ammunition, plus a provisions-train of 75 railway wagons. One train escaped – having steam raised when the cavalry charged the station, it pulled out with Dragoons in hot pursuit, firing from the saddle at the engine-driver who crouched in his cab and escaped being hit; the train gradually drew away and the mortified cavalry eventually brought their panting horses to a standstill, and shook their fists at the departing train.

The village of Tel el-Maskhuta was deserted and the infantry went into camp there, with a battalion of Guards going on to Mahsama. On this day, 25 August, the Bengal Lancers, 19th Hussars and the artillery of the India Contingent, now coming up

from Suez, made their disembarkation at Ismailia.

Commanded by Raschid Pasha, the Egyptian force defending the Mahsama – Tel el-Maskhuta area consisted of ten battalions of infantry, totalling 8,000 men; six squadrons of cavalry; 20 guns; and a large force of Bedouin.

The Advance to Kassassin Lock

An order for Kassassin Lock to be occupied by General Graham's brigade, who were to entrench it, was sent from Headquarters at 8 p.m. on 25 August and received by General Willis at 1.30 a.m. on the 26th; General Willis sent this order forward to General Graham, who had already left camp with the Royal Marines and Marine Artillery. Simultaneously the two other regiments of his brigade were sent forward to him and, at dawn on 26 August, General Graham, with the Yorks &

◄ *Mounted Infantry skirmishing ahead of the main force in the Kassassin area.*

▶ *Top right: the operations around Kassassin on 25-8 August 1882. An infantry skirmishing party moves along the railway embankment.*

▶ *Below right: Mahmoud Fehmy, Arabi's Chief of Staff, who was captured at Kassassin on 25 August 1882 when his scouting train went back to Tel el-Kebir without him.*

Lancs, DCLI and the Royal Marines, marched into the cavalry camp at Mahsama. Kassassin Lock, having been reconnoitred and found abandoned, was occupied by a detachment of the 4th Dragoons at daylight on 26 August; later in the day General Graham's Brigade moved forward and occupied the Lock area.

On 25 August while General Drury Lowe was surveying the village of Kassassin, a 'respectable-looking' Egyptian began conversing with him, in French. A captured Egyptian officer, passing under escort, cried out, 'That man is Mahmoud Fehmy – Arabi's second-in-command!' He admitted that he was indeed Fehmy and was immediately arrested. An important military figure, Fehmy Pasha designed the lines of entrenchment at Kafr ed-Dauar and Tel el-Kebir, where he was nominally adviser to Raschid Bey who commanded troops there, although *de facto* Fehmy was the commander. Scouting the area and left behind when his train returned to Tel el-Kebir without him, Fehmy Pasha conversed freely with his captors, revealing

British dispositions on 26 August

At Kassassin:
York & Lancs Regiment; Duke of Cornwall's Light Infantry; Royal Marine Artillery; two guns of the Royal Horse Artillery.

At Mahsama:
The Household Cavalry, 4th and 7th Dragoons, 3rd Bengal Cavalry, 30th Bengal Lancers and the Mounted Infantry.

At Tel el-Maskhuta:
Three Regiments of Guards, KRRC, a company of Royal Engineers, eight Royal Artillery guns.

At Nefisha:
Royal West Kent Regiment.

At Ismailia:
Three companies of Royal Engineers, seven guns.

that there were five field batteries of Krupp guns and three other batteries in position at Tel el-Kebir.

Considering the scale and scope of the engagements on 24–5 August, British losses of six men killed and 27 wounded were remarkably light, but a large number of men were laid-up by sunstroke and heat exhaustion: Household Cavalry 1 man killed, twelve wounded; Royal Horse Artillery three men killed, one wounded; York & Lancaster Regiment one man killed, six wounded; Royal Marine Artillery one man killed; Mounted Infantry two officers wounded; 7th Dragoon Guards one officer and five men wounded.

When Wolseley trans-shipped the expeditionary force from Alexandria to Ismailia, he left troops behind to guard the city and the lines at Ramleh under the command of General Sir Edward Hamley. This force proceeded to make its presence felt, engaging in numerous minor actions designed to keep the enemy occupied.

Officer of the Coldstream Guards on arrival in Egypt. Helmets were subsequently stained brown. He wears the 'Sam Browne' belt with revolver holster, pouch, sword frog and braces. (Michael Roffe)

Hamley's force at Ramleh

1 Brigade General Sir Archibald Alison
one Bn Royal Highlanders
two Bns Highland Light Infantry
two Bns Gordon Highlanders
two Bns Cameron Highlanders

2 Brigade General Sir Evelyn Wood
one Bn Sussex Regiment
one Bn Berkshire Regiment
one Bn South Staffordshire Regiment
one Bn The King's (Shropshire Light Infantry)

Plus divisional troops (cavalry, artillery, Royal Engineers, ancillary units).

The Action at Kassassin

General Graham's position at Kassassin Lock was not ideal for a small defensive force, but it was vital for the passage of boats and security of the canal that the lock be secured. On Monday 28 August, after enemy movements and gunfire earlier in the day, including cavalry appearing on hills to his right front, Graham signalled to the cavalry at Mahsama, who turned out and waited to be called forward, standing by their horses throughout a very hot day without shade or cover. Finally, as the enemy seemed to have given up the idea of an attack, they stood down in mid-afternoon, unsaddled their horses and returned to camp where they prepared a meal. But at about 4.30 the Egyptian artillery opened a heavy fire, and lines of skirmishers were seen advancing over a frontage of about a mile, evidently seeking to overlap Graham's left. His dispositions were as follows.

On the left, on the south side of the canal where low-lying ground deterred an Egyptian attack, were the Marine Artillery, who could protect the north and west of their position with a sweeping, flanking fire; about 800 yards to the east and at right-angles to them, were the DCLI, three companies thrown forward in extended order with supports and reserves under cover of the railway embankment; to their right-rear was echeloned the York & Lancaster Regiment, 2½ companies extended forward in skirmishing order, with the remainder of the battalion in support; the Mounted Infantry and a small dismounted force of 4th Dragoon Guards occupied the 800-yard interval between the Marine Artillery and the DCLI; on the extreme right was a troop of the 7th Dragoon Guards, with two 13pdrs plus two more that had been sent forward from the rear.

With the left perfectly protected by the nature of the position and the disposition of the units, the right would be effectively covered by the advance of cavalry from Mahsama, to whom Graham sent a warning message in order that they might very effectively catch the advancing enemy in open ground, should they attempt to turn his right.

During the rapid advance of the previous days, the difficulty of getting the guns forward through deep sand had necessitated using wagon-horses to supplement the limber-horses, so the ammunition-wagons had been left behind, and now the 13pdr guns, having performed sterling work against the advancing Egyptians, quickly ran out of ammunition. Only one gun remained firing, the action being adequately described in General Graham's dispatch.

'Near the right of our position, on the line of railway, a Krupp gun taken from the enemy at Mahsama had been mounted on railway track, and was being worked by a gun detachment of the Royal Marine Artillery, under Captain Tucker. This gun was admirably served, and did great execution among the enemy. As our other guns had to cease firing for want of ammunition, Captain Tucker's gun became a target for the enemy's artillery, and I counted salvoes of four guns opening-up on him with shell and shrapnel; but although everything around was hit, not a man of the detachment was touched, and this gun continued to fire to the end, expending ninety-three rounds.'

At about 5.30 Graham sent his aide-de-camp, Lieutenant Pirie, 4th Dragoon Guards, with an order to General Drury Lowe: 'Take the cavalry round by our right, under cover of the hill, and attack the left flank of the enemy's skirmishers.'

But Pirie had difficulty finding the cavalry which had moved back to camp after a tiring day, and eventually had to obtain a horse from an artillery battery when his own fell exhausted. Aware that General Graham's plans hinged on the cavalry charging on the right, Pirie gave General Drury Lowe a different message, saying that Graham 'was only just able to hold his own, and wished the cavalry to attack the left of the enemy's infantry skirmishers'.

At about 7.15 p.m., his left and front secured by the arrival of a battalion of Royal Marines and six guns, and confident that his right was covered by the cavalry charge he had ordered, Graham sent his troops forward in a general advance, moving evenly in echelon from the left, firing steady volleys by successive companies. In this way the formation went forward for 2 or 3 miles, the enemy falling back before them, after making only one attempt to stand. But by now it was night and in the dark mistakes could be made, so at 8.45 the troops retired on their camp.

British dispositions on 28 August

At Kassassin under General Graham

4th Dragoon Guards	15 men
7th Dragoon Guards	42 men
Duke of Cornwall's Light Infantry	611 men
Mounted Infantry	70 men
Royal Marine Artillery	427 men
N/A Battery RHA	2 guns, 40 men

At Mahsama under General Drury Lowe

I Cavalry Brigade commanded by Sir Baker Russell	
Household Cavalry	3 squadrons
7th Dragoon Guards	
N/A Battery, RHA	4 guns
G/B Battery, RHA	2 guns
Royal Marine Light Infantry	

At Tel el-Maskhuta

4th Dragoon Guards	
19th Hussars	2 squadrons
D/I Battery RA	4 guns
Brigade of Guards	
3rd Bn, King's Royal Rifle Corps	

Later arrivals

Royal West Kent Regiment
I/2 and N/2 Batteries, RA

Three contemporary illustrations depicting the charge of the Household Cavalry (one squadron each of 1st Life Guards, 2nd Life Guards and Royal Horse Guards) at Kassassin on 28 August 1882. Led by Brigadier Baker Russell and Colonel Ewart, and flanked by Dragoons, they destroyed enemy infantry, but it is doubtful whether they ever actually got among the guns, authoritative sources claiming that they missed them in the twilight.

The sun had set and a bright moon was shining as the tired horses advanced as fast as the heavy terrain would permit, guided by the flashes from guns to their left-front, although later the 7th Dragoon Guards claimed to have moved on the evening star. Through the grey sand, with dust-clouds and desert haze rendering the moon indistinct, Drury Lowe took his weary cavalry round in a wide sweep to turn the enemy left, keeping a sand ridge between them until the moment came to charge. Suddenly they found themselves exposed to fierce artillery fire, mostly too high to do any damage and, by moving right, the enemy aim was disturbed. General Drury Lowe ordered the 7th Dragoons, in the van, to wheel outwards, thus clearing the front for the Royal Horse Artillery guns to open fire; they then re-formed in rear of the guns and the Household Cavalry. Drury Lowe gave the order to charge; Brigadier Baker Russell, out in front of the élite troopers on their big black horses, cried loudly: 'Trot!', 'Gallop!', 'Charge!' Flanked by the Dragoons, the Household Cavalry cascaded down on the enemy infantry, taking them partly in front and in flank, to annihilate them. In his official dispatch, Drury Lowe said:

'The enemy's infantry were completely scattered, and our cavalry swept on, through a battery of seven or nine guns, which in daylight must have been captured, but unfortunately their exact position could not be found afterwards and they were no doubt removed during the night after our retirement. The enemy's loss was heavy, the ground being strewn thickly with their killed, and quantities of ammunition, etc.'

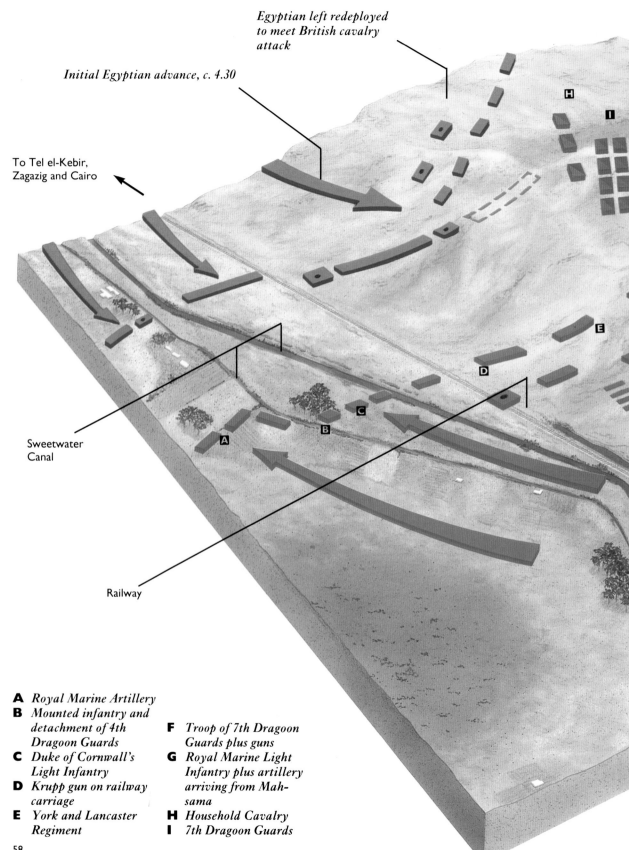

Egyptian left redeployed to meet British cavalry attack

Initial Egyptian advance, c. 4.30

To Tel el-Kebir, Zagazig and Cairo

H

I

E

D

C

B

A

Sweetwater Canal

Railway

A *Royal Marine Artillery*
B *Mounted infantry and detachment of 4th Dragoon Guards*
C *Duke of Cornwall's Light Infantry*
D *Krupp gun on railway carriage*
E *York and Lancaster Regiment*
F *Troop of 7th Dragoon Guards plus guns*
G *Royal Marine Light Infantry plus artillery arriving from Mah-sama*
H *Household Cavalry*
I *7th Dragoon Guards*

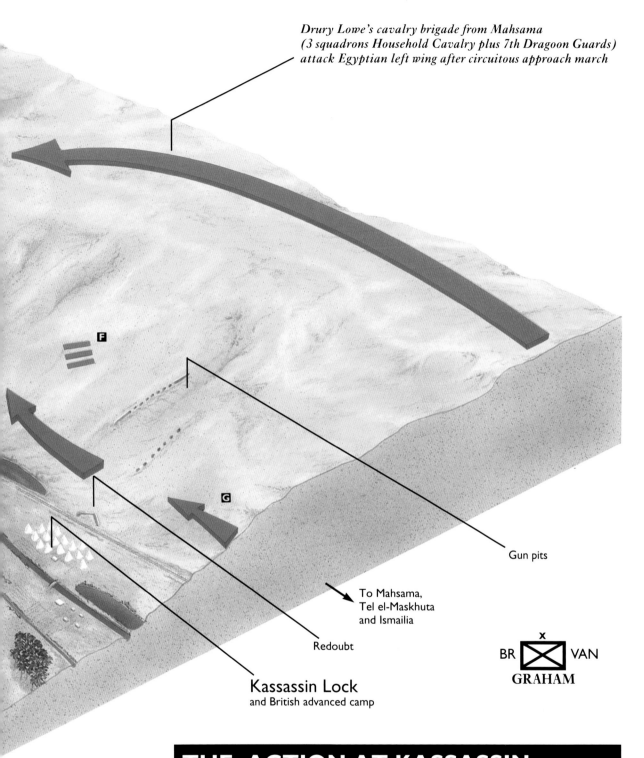

*Drury Lowe's cavalry brigade from Mahsama
(3 squadrons Household Cavalry plus 7th Dragoon Guards)
attack Egyptian left wing after circuitous approach march*

F

G

Gun pits

To Mahsama,
Tel el-Maskhuta
and Ismailia

Redoubt

BR VAN
GRAHAM

Kassassin Lock
and British advanced camp

THE ACTION AT KASSASSIN

28 August 1882: showing the situation at the end of the British advance, as seen from the south-east

▲ *After the Battle of Kassassin, seeking and succouring the dead and wounded of both sides.*

British Casualties on 28 August	Killed		Wounded	
	Officers	NCOs & men	Officers	NCOs & men
Graham's Force:				
4th Dragoon Guards				1
Mounted Infantry			2	5
Royal Marine Artillery		6	3	21
Duke of Cornwall's Light Infantry			4	14
3rd Bn King's Royal Rifle Corps			1	
2nd Bn Yorks & Lancs		1		9
Army Medical Dept	1			
Army Hospital Corps				1
Total	1	7	10	51
Mahsama Force				
1st Life Guards		6		5
2nd Life Guards			1	1
Royal Horse Guards		1		7
7th Dragoon Guards	1	1		3
Commissariat & Transport Corps				1
Total	1	8	1	17

To the left-rear of the Egyptian infantry was a body of cavalry which did not attempt to charge but made off when British cavalry neared them, although Egyptian reports indicate otherwise. It is interesting to note that, although much was made of the Household Cavalry's charging the guns, Colonel J. F. Maurice's definitive book on the war states conclusively that all evidence, both Egyptian and British, indicates that the cavalry never reached the guns, having failed to find them in the darkness. However, this cavalry charge successfully ended the day's actions, with the enemy surrendering the field to the British.

General Graham estimated that the enemy forces in action during 28 August were in the region of 8,000 cavalry, 1,000 infantry and twelve guns. There is little record of Egyptian losses, although a correspondent present at the battle believed that about 400 were killed, and numerous wounded were brought in by the British.

The Commander-in-Chief, Sir Garnet Wolseley, arrived at Kassassin shortly after the fight, and was soon joined by strong reinforcements – the bulk of 1st Division and the India Contingent – for the march inland. At Ismailia stores and equipment were being feverishly landed; the railway was working to a schedule; and the service of steamboats along the canal brought in all that was required for the offensive.

British Reinforcements

On 29 August orders from Wolseley were received in Alexandria detailing General Sir Archibald Alison's 1 Highland Brigade to embark for Ismailia, to join the main army for the major battles to come. General Sir Edward Hamley, with his Staff, was also to go; leaving General Sir Evelyn Wood and his 2 Brigade guarding the city and the lines at Ramleh. Embarking on 30 August in the transports *Lusitania*, *Iberia*, and *British Prince*, the force arrived at Ismailia at 6 p.m. on 1 September. The men were kept on the ships, only disembarking during the day for fatigue duties and work-parties; they did not finally disembark until 9 September.

The Highlanders, in fighting order of kilt, red serge (jacket), brown helmet, waist-belt, three ball-bags, water-bottle, haversack, and 100 rounds per man, set out to march the 21 miles to Kassassin. The Gordons led, followed by the Camerons, then the Highland Light Infantry and finally, the Black Watch – all marching in mass of columns at one-pace intervals, with cavalry on one flank and artillery on the other. It was an extremely hard march under blazing sun over a soft sandy desert; despite taking four days over it, many men fell out and at least one death from sunstroke was recorded.

On 28 August General MacPherson's India Contingent arrived at Ismailia and the army was reorganized, the units being redistributed as listed in the table overleaf.

Renewed Action at Kassassin

In the days following the fight on 28 August, troops were moved forward as quickly as possible, to mass at Kassassin preparatory to moving on the lines at Tel el-Kebir. During this period scattered parties of Bedouin prowled the area and, seeking to find favour with Arabi for their activities, gave him to understand that not only was Kassassin weakly held, but that they had cut off communication between that place and Ismailia. Subsequently Arabi decided to make a combined attack with forces from Tel el-Kebir and Salahieh and, early on the morning of 9 September, a long line of Egyptian soldiers was seen marching down towards Kassassin from the west and north-west, their white uniforms showing clearly in the horizontal rays of the rising sun.

Towards the north the ridges were crowded with them, and dense masses could be seen on the south bank of the canal. *The Army and Navy Gazette* reported that Arabi himself was leading 13,000 infantry, besides Regular cavalry, Bedouin, and a great deal of artillery from Tel el-Kebir; while from Salahieh a strong column was variously reported as numbering from 1,500 to 5,000 men. *The Times* correspondent estimated that the Egyptian commander was leading 8,000 men with 24 guns.

The attack was first discovered at about 5 a.m. by outpost patrols of the 13th Bengal Lancers who, after sending back riders to warn the camp, made a fighting retreat. Soon the enemy were on the sandhills, working steadily round Graham's right flank; columns of steam rising in the misty air indicated trains coming up from Tel el-Kebir. The alarm was

Organization of the British expeditionary Force after 28 August

FIRST DIVISION

1 Brigade
2nd Bn Grenadier Guards
2nd Bn Coldstream Guards
1st Bn Scots Guards
Naval Brigade

2 Brigade
2nd Bn Royal Irish Fusiliers
1st Bn Royal West Kent Regiment
Royal Marine Light Infantry
2nd Bn York & Lancaster Regiment
1st Bn Royal Irish Fusiliers

Divisional Troops
19th Hussars (2 squadrons)
2nd Bn DCLI
A/1 Royal Artillery
D/1 Royal Artillery
24th Coy, Royal Engineers
12th Coy, Commissariat & Transport
½ No. 1 Bearer Company
No. 3 Field Hospital

SECOND DIVISION

3 Brigade
1st Bn Royal Highlanders
1st Bn Gordon Highlanders
1st Bn Cameron Highlanders
2nd Bn Highland Light Infantry

India Contingent (attached)
7/1 (Mountain Battery)
1st Bn Manchester Regiment
1st Bn Seaforth Highlanders
7th Bengal Infantry

20th Punjab Infantry
29th Baluchis
Medical Dept, Ambulance, etc.
Transport
Commissariat
RE Field Park
Ordnance Department

Divisional Troops
19th Hussars (2 squadrons)
3rd Bn King's Royal Rifles
I/2 Royal Artillery
N/2
26th Coy, Royal Engineers
11th Coy, Commissariat & Transport
½ No. 2 Bearer Company
Nos. 4 & 5 Field Hospitals
No. 2 Field Hospital (attached)

CAVALRY DIVISION

1 Brigade
Household Cavalry (3 squadrons)
4th Dragoon Guards
7th Dragoon Guards
17th Coy, Commissariat & Transport
(part of)
½ No. 1 Bearer Company

2 Brigade
2nd Bengal Cavalry
6th Bengal Cavalry
13th Bengal Lancers

Divisional Troops
N/A Royal Horse Artillery
Mounted Infantry

Detachment, RE
17th Coy, Commissariat & Transport
(part of)
No. 6 Field Hospital

CORPS TROOPS

Corps Artillery
G/B Royal Horse Artillery
H1 Royal Artillery
C/3 Royal Artillery
J/3 Royal Artillery
F/1 Royal Artillery (ammunition
column)
Royal Marine Artillery

Siege Train
1st Bn London Regiment
5th Bn Scottish Regiment
6th Bn Scottish Regiment

ORDNANCE STORES DEPARTMENT

Corps Engineers
'A' (Pontoon) Troop
'C' (Telegraph) Troop
Field Park
8th, 17th & 18th Coys
Railway Staff
Queen's Own Sappers & Miners
(A and I Companies)
Commissariat & Transport
(8, 15 and aux Coys)
No. 2 Bearer Company
Nos. 1, 7 & 8 Field Hospitals

◀ *The British camp at Kassassin during the last days of August and early September 1882. The artist has marked salient features: 1. Enemy vedettes in distance; 2. The distant lines of Tel el-Kebir; 3. Enemy vedettes; 4. The Freshwater Canal. 5. The railway; 6. Horses going to water; 7. Enemy vedette; 8. Camp of 60th Rifles [KRRC]; 9. Drawbridge and lock; 10. Hussar's camp, with smoke of railway engine in rear; 11. British vedettes. The area forming the background to this illustration is the actual field over which the actions at Kassassin were fought.*

sounded at 6.45 a.m. and by 7.10 the troops were formed in order of battle, as shells began to burst in and around the camp, exploding among the tents and throwing dust high in the air, causing horses and cattle to break their halters and run wild through the canvas streets.

On the south bank of the canal Graham deployed the Royal Marine Artillery and five companies of the Royal West Kent Regiment, with two 25pdr guns served by 5th Battery, Scottish Division, RA. On the north bank, the King's Royal Rifle Corps had their left resting on the canal; the Royal Marines took up the line from them, with Yorks & Lancs on the Marines' right, their right somewhat thrown back. Two field batteries, 'A' and 'D', 1 Brigade, RA, with 16pdrs, were placed in previously constructed gun-pits on the north of the camp, facing the enemy advance from the west; they were in position by 7 a.m. The Royal Irish were to their right, their right thrown back to present an infantry front against the Salahieh force; immediately after the action began, they were reinforced by the Duke of Cornwall's Light Infantry from the south bank.

At 6.45 a.m. Drury Lowe ordered the whole of the Indian Cavalry Brigade to turn out and delay the enemy; at 7.10 1 Cavalry Brigade under Sir Baker Russell also moved out of camp; G/B Battery RHA accompanied the Indian Brigade, while N/A went with 1 Cavalry Brigade. The cavalry force rode out far to the right of the camp and, by threatening the

Corporal of Horse, the Life Guards. He carries the special Household Cavalry pattern sword; haversack and water bottle were carried on straps crossing the chest. (Michael Roffe)

Egyptian left, hampered their flanking movements. Simultaneously the enemy cavalry rode out parallel with Drury Lowe's force, each attempting to flank the other and occasionally halting as artillery came into action.

Meanwhile the British artillery had begun to come into play and, although inferior in numbers, gradually obtained the mastery. The enemy infantry had advanced on each side of the canal and railway and on the slopes of the sandhills, and were maintaining a continuous rifle-fire from 800 yards' range. At 7.45 a general advance was ordered against them. The Marines and Royal Rifle Corps went forward along the line of the canal and railway, as the Yorks & Lancs moved forward against those Egyptian troops descending the slopes and, with the rest of the infantry in support, the three battalions came into action against eighteen Egyptian infantry regiments. The rolling crackle of musketry was continuous and heavy, but the more numerous enemy could not withstand the British fire, now augmented to six

▲ *Indian Cavalry. Bengal Lancers, forming part of General Wilkinson's 2 Cavalry Brigade of General Drury Lowe's Cavalry Division. It was a party of 30 men of this brigade who, on 9 September, went out with Colonel Pennington (13th Bengal Lancers) to post vedettes and, on seeing*

three squadrons of cavalry with infantry advancing towards the camp, engaged them.

▶ *Above right: a general view of the action in front of Kassassin on 9 September 1882*

regiments as the supporting troops came forward.

Graham's forces continued to move forward until 10.30 a.m. by which time the Egyptians were in hasty retreat, leaving behind three guns, two taken by the Royal Marines and one by the Riflemen; and British troops had arrived within 5,000 yards of the Tel el-Kebir fortifications. It was said that General Buller, who had accompanied the cavalry, was actually in consultation with General Drury Lowe as to the advisability of pushing a force

forward to Zagazig, when specific orders forbidding such a move were received from Sir Garnet Wolseley.

The extent of the enemy's losses is not known, although it was reported that the Royal Horse Artillery, with the cavalry force on the flank, killed or wounded about 70. Most reports mention many prisoners being taken.

More Troops Arrive at Kassassin

The Guards Brigade had started from Tel el–Maskhuta early in the day, ordered by General Willis to try and fall upon the left flank of the enemy force from Salahieh; but events had moved too quickly for this to be possible and, after a trying and wearisome march, they arrived at the camp at 4 p.m. The four regiments of the Highland Brigade marched in next morning; troops continued to arrive, the last to take their place being the Royal Irish Fusiliers in the afternoon of 12 September.

British Casualties, 9 September

	Killed		Wounded	
	Officers	Men	Officers	Men
'G' Battery, 'B' Brigade, RHA				1
2nd Bengal Cavalry				2
13th Lancers		1		1
'N' Battery, 'A' Brigade, RHA				2
2nd Royal Irish Regiment				2
Royal Marine Light Infantry				25
2nd Yorks & Lancs Regiment				6
Staff, Royal Artillery				
'A' Battery, 1 Brigade, RA				3
'D' Battery, 1 Brigade, RA				5
3rd King's Royal Rifles		2		25
Staff			1	
Royal Navy			1	
Total	0	3	2	75

The Battle of Tel el-Kebir, 9 September 1882

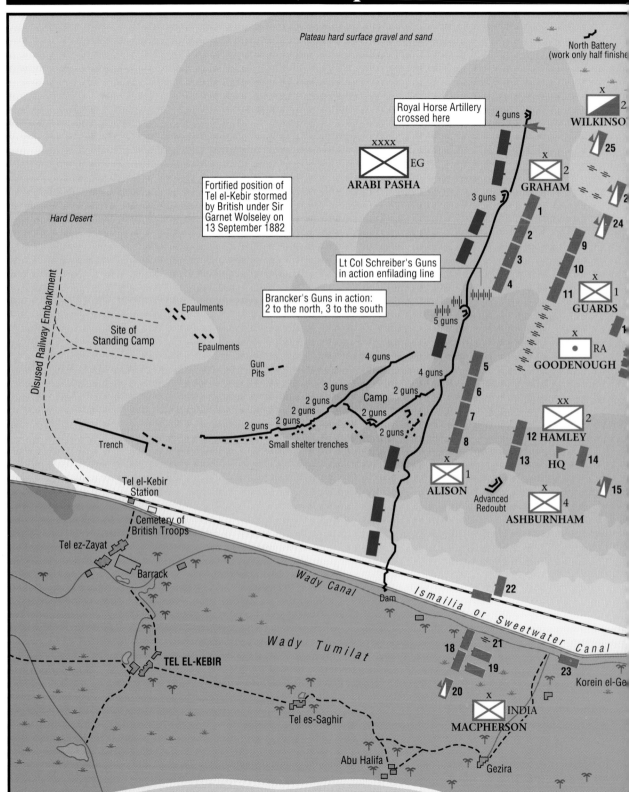

Plateau hard surface gravel and sand

North Battery
(work only half finishe

WILKINSO

Royal Horse Artillery
crossed here

4 guns

25

XXXX
EG
ARABI PASHA

2
GRAHAM

3 guns

Fortified position of
Tel el-Kebir stormed
by British under Sir
Garnet Wolseley on
13 September 1882

Hard Desert

1

2

24

3

9

10

Lt Col Schreiber's Guns
in action enfilading line

4

11

GUARDS

Brancker's Guns in action:
2 to the north, 3 to the south

5 guns

RA
GOODENOUGH

Epaulments

Site of
Standing Camp

Epaulments

Gun
Pits

4 guns

4 guns

3 guns

2 guns

5

XX
2

2 guns

6

2 guns

Camp

2 guns

7

12 HAMLEY

2 guns

2 guns

2 guns

8

13

HQ

14

Trench

Small shelter trenches

2 guns

1
ALISON

15

Tel el-Kebir
Station

Advanced
Redoubt

4
ASHBURNHAM

Cemetery of
British Troops

Tel ez-Zayat

Barrack

Wady Canal

Dam

Ismailia or Sweetwater Canal

22

Wady Tumilat

18

21

TEL EL-KEBIR

19

23

Korein el-Ge

20

Tel es-Saghir

INDIA
MACPHERSON

Abu Halifa

Gezira

Disused Railway Embankment

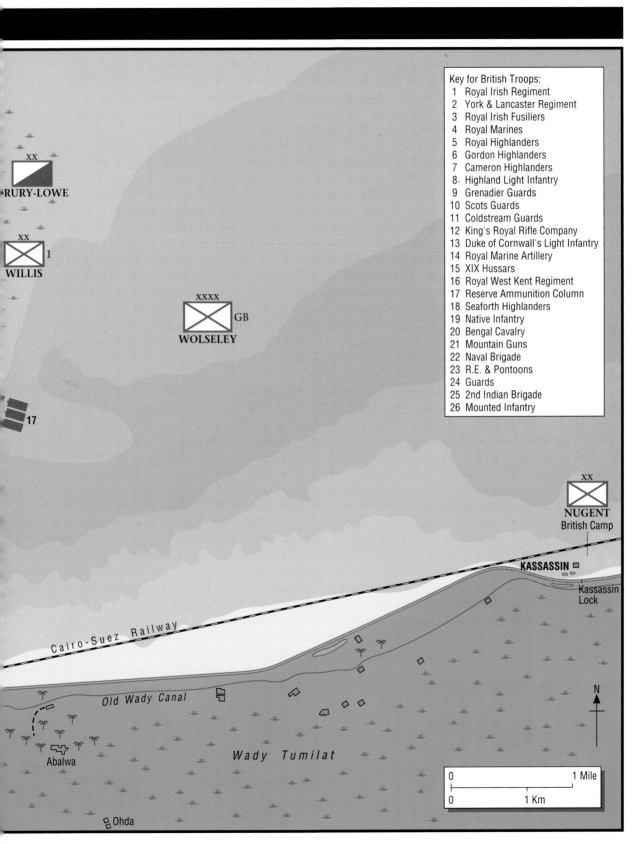

Key for British Troops:
1 Royal Irish Regiment
2 York & Lancaster Regiment
3 Royal Irish Fusiliers
4 Royal Marines
5 Royal Highlanders
6 Gordon Highlanders
7 Cameron Highlanders
8 Highland Light Infantry
9 Grenadier Guards
10 Scots Guards
11 Coldstream Guards
12 King's Royal Rifle Company
13 Duke of Cornwall's Light Infantry
14 Royal Marine Artillery
15 XIX Hussars
16 Royal West Kent Regiment
17 Reserve Ammunition Column
18 Seaforth Highlanders
19 Native Infantry
20 Bengal Cavalry
21 Mountain Guns
22 Naval Brigade
23 R.E. & Pontoons
24 Guards
25 2nd Indian Brigade
26 Mounted Infantry

THE BATTLE OF TEL EL-KEBIR

During the evening of the 11th, Sir Garnet Wolseley and his Staff had arrived and reconnaissance of the enemy's positions began at dawn next day.

Wolseley and his Staff would have seen before them a line of entrenchments some four miles long, extending from the canal towards el Karain in the desert; on its other bank soft earthworks, with hurdle revetments. These works, on which thousands of *fellahin* had laboured for weeks, had a frontage of 6,600 yards, but the intended inundation did not seem to have been carried out by Arabi. At intervals along the line, connected by trenches, were gun redoubts with front and rear fields of fire. Supporting the front line were other redoubts, particularly strong toward the right-centre of the position by virtue of crowning eminences and the fact that they had been constructed with considerable skill. Similar works covered the flanks in the form of an entrenched line and armed redoubts; these were considered to be unassailable by cavalry.

Egyptian Troop Dispositions at Tel el-Kebir

According to Arabi Pasha's subsequent statement made when he was in exile in Ceylon, his forces holding the lines of Tel el-Kebir – 20,000 strong with 75 guns – were disposed as given below.

At a point situated between Tel el-Kebir and Kassassin, about 2,300 yards east of the works of Tel el-Kebir: one infantry battalion and four guns. Farther south, at Abu Nishaba, on sandhills at the edge of the desert and wadi: 4½ miles from Kassassin: two infantry battalions, 2,000 Bedouin, 300 cavalry and two guns. At the dam immediately in the rear of the southernmost point of the entrenchments: three infantry battalions and six guns. At the advanced work in front of the entrenchments: one infantry battalion and four guns. Occupying the lines of the entrenchments: 54

guns and ten infantry battalions: six along the southern sector of the front face, three on their left, i.e. to the north, and one yet farther to the left, to the extreme north. In reserve: three infantry battalions, five guns and the remainder of the cavalry (1,700). (The total numbers given in the first part of Arabi's statement do not tally with British Intelligence at the time, who believed that there were 25,000 men, or 30,000 including the Bedouin.) Arabi also added that all regimental officers were with their men; superior officers sleeping close behind them and the Commander, Ali Rubi Pasha, slept in Arabi's tent.

British Preparations for the Battle

During the afternoon of the 12th orders were given that the force would march that night to attack the enemy within the lines of Tel el-Kebir. All tents were to be struck by 6.30 p.m., and all baggage to be piled alongside the railway opposite the camps of its owners, ready for transporting to the rear. The troops would then march to predetermined areas, halt and bivouack until ordered to fall-in for the advance. Each soldier would carry 100 rounds of ammunition and rations for two days; water-bottles would be filled with tea. Regimental transports would carry two days' full rations and 30 rounds of reserve ammunition per man.

The 40pdr gun on the railway truck, which had rendered such good service on 9 September, was to have the Naval Brigade attached; the seven batteries of the Royal Artillery were to form one artillery brigade under General Goodenough; the two horse artillery batteries would be attached to the cavalry with whom it was planned to make a detour and come down on the rear of the enemy's position.

In his dispatch from Ismailia on 13 September (after the battle) Sir Garnet Wolseley outlined his intentions:

BRITISH ORDER OF BATTLE AT TEL EL-KEBIR

CAVALRY DIVISION

Commanding: Major-General D.C. Drury Lowe, CB

1 Brigade
Brigadier-General Sir Baker Russell, KCMG, CB
three Squadrons Household Cavalry
one Squadron 1st Life Guards
one Squadron 2nd Life Guards
one Squadron Royal Horse Guards
4th Dragoon Guards
7th Dragoon Guards
17th Coy Commissariat & Transport Corps
½ Bearer Company
1,590 men, 1,350 horses

2 Brigade
Brigadier-General H.C. Wilkinson
13th Bengal Lancers
2nd Bengal Cavalry
6th Bengal Cavalry
1,497 men, 1,590 horses

Divisional Troops
N/A Battery Royal Horse Artillery
Mounted Infantry

FIRST DIVISION

Lieutenant-General G.H.S. Willis, CB

1 Brigade
Major-General H.R.H. the Duke of Connaught, KT, KP, GCSI, GCMG
2nd Bn Grenadier Guards
2nd Bn Coldstream Guards
1st Bn Scots Guards

2 Brigade
Major-General Gerald Graham, VC, CB, RE
Royal Marine Liht Infantry

1st Bn Royal West Kent Regiment
2nd Bn York and Lancaster Regiment
1st Bn Royal Irish Fusiliers

Divisional Troops
19th Hussars (two squadrons)
'A' Battery, 1 Brigade Royal Artillery
'D' Battery, 1 Brigade Royal Artillery
24th Coy Royal Engineers
11th Coy Commissariat & Transport
½ Bearer Company
Two Field Hospitals
Postal Department

SECOND DIVISION

Lieutenant-General Sir Edward Hamley, KCMG, CB, RA

1 Brigade
Major-General Sir Archibald Alison, KCB
1st Bn Royal Highlanders
2nd Bn Highland Light Infantry
1st Bn Gordon Highlanders
1st Bn Cameron Highlanders

4 Brigade
Colonel C. Ashburnham
2nd Bn Duke of Cornwall's Light Infantry
3rd Bn King's Royal Rifle Corps

Divisional Troops
19th Hussars (two squadrons)
'I' Battery, 2 Brigade, Royal Artillery
'N' Battery, 2 Brigade, Royal Artillery
26th Coy Royal Engineers
Veterinary Department
12th Coy Commissariat & Transport
½ Bearer Company
Two Field Hospitals
Postal Department

CORPS TROOPS

Artillery Corps
'G' Battery, 'B' Brigade, Royal Horse Artillery
'C' Battery, 3 Brigade, Royal Artillery
'T' Battery, 3 Brigade, Royal Artillery
Ammunition Reserve, Royal Artillery
'F' Battery, 1 Brigade, Royal Artillery

Siege Train
4th and 5th Batteries, London Division, Royal Artillery
5th and 6th Batteries, Scottish Division, Royal Artillery

INDIA CONTINGENT

Major-General Sir Herbert Macpherson, VC, KCB, BSc

Infantry Brigade
Brigadier-General, O.V. Tanner, CB
1st Bn Seaforth Highlanders (Ross-shire Buffs; the Duke of Albany's)
7th Bengal Native Infantry
20th Bengal (Punjab) Native Infantry
29th Company (2nd Baluchi) Native Infantry

Artillery
'H' Battery, 1 Brigade, Royal Artillery
7th Battery, 1 Brigade, Northern Division, Royal Artillery (Mountain Battery)

Engineers
'A' and 'I' Companies Madras (Queen's Own) Sappers & Miners

Additional Infantry Battalion
1st Bn Manchester Regiment

'I struck camp at Kassassin Lock yesterday evening. After bivouacking on the high ridge above the camp until 1.30 this morning, I then advanced upon the very extensive and very strongly fortified positions held by Arabi. My force was about 11,000 bayonets, 2,000 sabres and 60 guns.

'To have attacked such a position by daylight with the troops I could place in the line would have entailed very great loss. I resolved therefore to attack before daybreak, doing the six miles that intervened between my camp and the enemy's position in the dark.'

The Order of Advance

On the left was General Hamley's 2nd Division; leading the advance was Alison's Brigade, moving in half-battalion columns of double companies; on the left flank nearest the canal, 2nd Battalion Highland Light Infantry; 1st Battalion Cameron Highlanders;

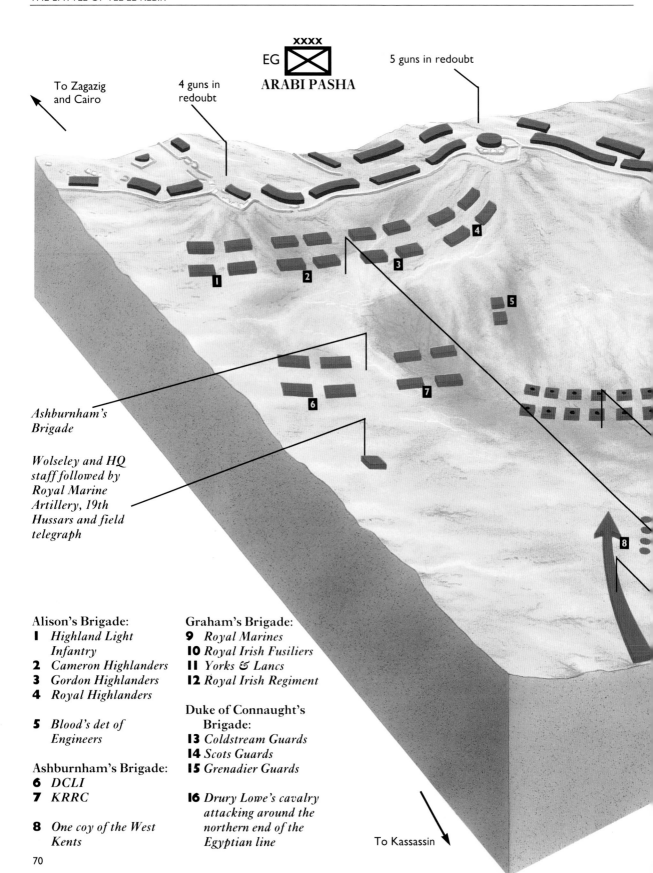

EG **XXXX** ☒
ARABI PASHA

4 guns in
redoubt

5 guns in redoubt

To Zagazig
and Cairo

1

2

3

4

5

6

7

8

*Ashburnham's
Brigade*

*Wolseley and HQ
staff followed by
Royal Marine
Artillery, 19th
Hussars and field
telegraph*

Alison's Brigade:
1 *Highland Light
   Infantry*
2 *Cameron Highlanders*
3 *Gordon Highlanders*
4 *Royal Highlanders*

5 *Blood's det of
   Engineers*

Ashburnham's Brigade:
6 *DCLI*
7 *KRRC*

8 *One coy of the West
   Kents*

Graham's Brigade:
9 *Royal Marines*
10 *Royal Irish Fusiliers*
11 *Yorks & Lancs*
12 *Royal Irish Regiment*

**Duke of Connaught's
   Brigade:**
13 *Coldstream Guards*
14 *Scots Guards*
15 *Grenadier Guards*

16 *Drury Lowe's cavalry
   attacking around the
   northern end of the
   Egyptian line*

To Kassassin

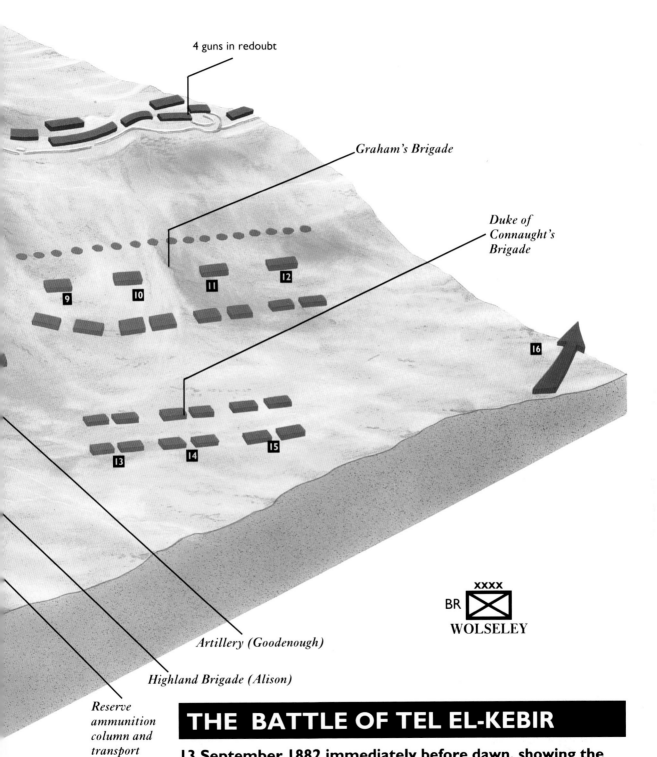

4 guns in redoubt

Graham's Brigade

Duke of
Connaught's
Brigade

9   10   11   12

13   14   15   16

BR XXXX WOLSELEY

Artillery (Goodenough)

Highland Brigade (Alison)

Reserve
ammunition
column and
transport

THE BATTLE OF TEL EL-KEBIR

13 September 1882 immediately before dawn, showing the British right wing and centre, after night approach march, in position for the attack; as seen from the south-east

1st Battalion Gordon Highlanders; and on the brigade's right flank, The Black Watch. In support, 1,000 yards behind them, was Ashburnham's 4 Brigade composed of King's Royal Rifle Corps and Duke of Cornwall's Light Infantry.

On the British right was Willis's 1st Division, with General Graham's Brigade leading the advance, in line of half-battalion columns of companies at deployed intervals, with Royal Irish Fusiliers on the Brigade's left; then Yorks & Lancs; Royal Marine Light Infantry; and on the right flank, the 2nd Battalion Royal Irish Regiment. Behind them in support, Duke of Connaught's Guards Brigade, from left to right 2nd Battalion Coldstream Guards; 1st Battalion Scots Guards; and 2nd Battalion Grenadier Guards.

Between the supporting Guards Brigade and 4 Brigade were positioned seven batteries (42 guns) Royal Artillery; and on the right of the Guards Brigade were twelve guns of the Royal Horse Artillery (two batteries); then on the far right flank of the entire army, Drury Lowe's Cavalry Division.

On the south side of the canal was General Macpherson's India Contingent, totalling 1,678 officers and men; it consisted of 1st Battalion Seaforth Highlanders; 7th Bengal Native Infantry; 20th Punjab Native Infantry; 29th Baluchi Native Infantry; one squadron 6th Bengal Cavalry; 7/1 Mountain Battery, Royal Artillery; a section of Sappers (seven officers, 248 men).

Attached to the contingent was Captain Fitzroy's Naval Brigade, 210 bluejackets with six Gatlings, who marched on the northern bank of the canal, while Macpherson's infantry advanced along the southern bank, contact between them being maintained by Royal Engineers' pontoons, moving on the canal and keeping pace with the Indian and Naval forces.

The strength of Wolseley's Force was:

CAVALRY:	125 officers	2,660 NCOs and men
INFANTRY:	422 officers	11,702 NCOs and men
ARTILLERY:	87 officers	2,405 NCOs and men
TOTAL:	634 officers	16,767 NCOs and men

plus 61 guns and 6 Gatlings.

The Night March to Tel el-Kebir

As the canal and the railway-line ran side-by-side through the British position, straight up to Arabi's entrenchments and through them, these formed the directing lines for Wolseley's advance, which began at 1.30 a.m. Macpherson's force was ordered not to leave until an hour later, and then to march directly along the bank of the canal which, it being easier and quicker than the desert march, would ensure that they would arrive after the attack had commenced, thus giving no early warning of its approach.

The night was very dark and forward movement was governed by the stars, Intelligence officers with compasses riding ahead; all who took part in the march later recalled the utter silence, broken only by the crunching of feet and wheels over the pebble-strewn sand and the jingle of chain-harness; frequent halts enabled contact to be maintained. Daylight was just breaking when the force arrived within 1,000 yards of the enemy parapets; a short halt allowed formations to close-up and final preparations to be made; the supporting brigades were brought up behind their forward brigades. Silence reigned and it was difficult to realize that 14,000 men stood ready to dash forward upon an apparently unprepared – and probably slumbering – enemy.

Drury Lowe's cavalry did not move out at the same time as the main body, nor on the same line, their aim being to sweep around the enemy rear at daybreak; first moving in a due northerly direction in column of troops, later they advanced on a north-westerly line, halting after two hours to front west, awaiting the sound of gunfire which would be their signal for advancing. The Division moved off in the order: 13th Bengal Lancers, followed in succession by 2nd Bengal Cavalry and 6th Bengal Cavalry; N/A and G/B Batteries, Royal Horse Artillery; the Heavy Brigade (Household Cavalry, Dragoons and Mounted Infantry) formed the rear of the column.

◀ *War artist Melton Prior's on-the-spot sketch of the Highland Brigade attacking on the left half of the British line, advan-* *cing over the open ground within the enemy's entrenchments.*

The infantry had marched towards the enemy lines with unloaded rifles and bayonets unfixed, and had been warned that there would be only two signals: the command 'Fix Bayonets' and, on reaching the defences, a bugle call 'to storm'. First came the sharp click as bayonets were clamped to rifles, without interrupting the slow measured tread across the sand. But then, when they were within 300 yards of the enemy lines, a single rifle-shot broke the silence, followed almost immediately by a torrent of wild fire flashing all along the parapets, sending a storm of bullets mostly over the heads of the attackers. At this moment, neither the Highland Brigade nor Graham's Brigade knew the exact position of each other, being unaware that the whole front of the army had assumed the form of an irregular echelon, with the Highland Brigade on the left thrown forward so that when they were within single charge distance, Graham's Brigade were still some 800–900 yards from the parapets. This meant that 2 Brigade had to advance over a longer belt of fire, which delayed them to the extent that the story of the taking of the enemy works during the first ten minutes of the battle was the story of the advance of the Highland Brigade.

The Attack of the Highland Brigade

Buglers sounded the advance and there was a cascade of cheering from the Highlanders who rushed forward in two long waves, the half-battalion double columns having closed-in on each other so that the brigade was formed in two nearly continuous lines. General Hamley, between these two lines, checked the advance of the rear companies of the Gordon and Cameron Highlanders, forming them into a support. Taking casualties from the heavy close-range fire, the men struggled through the loose sand of the steep scarp to the parapet above, groups forming to help one another on to the top at dispersed points. For a time the enemy fire was so heavy, the defenders standing their ground, that on the left of the two centre regiments – Gordons and Camerons – the attackers were driven back, but at other points groups sprang down on to the *terre-plein* below to establish a footing within the works. Even so, these groups, exposed to fire on three sides, began to give way; General Hamley now

brought forward the supports he had kept in hand and rallied the wavering troops upon them, personally leading them forward to strengthen those advancing on the farther side of the front trench. Mixed groups of Camerons, Gordons and Black Watch, under any officer there to lead them, pushed forward, attacking first one party of Egyptians and then another until the front rampart between the two higher batteries was won.

In the meantime, on their left the Highland Light Infantry had struggled in vain to cross the formidable ditch that fronted them, higher than in other parts of the line and manned by Nubian troops who fought with great courage. Seemingly they held their fire until the attackers were bunched in their attempts to scramble up the scarp then delivered close-range volleys before being led forward in a charge, their formed ranks driving back the scattered groups of Highland Light Infantry. On the right, The Black Watch had also found themselves facing a strong and well-defended work

▲ *A spirited drawing of the charge of the Highland Brigade at the Battle of Tel el-Kebir. The picture shows them approaching the Egyptian lines, before tackling the ditch and parapets.*

▶ *Entitled 'First in the Fray', this sketch by a special war artist graced the cover of* **The Illustrated London News** *on 7 October 1882. It depicts the storming of the Egyptian parapet and gun emplacements by men of Alison's Highland Brigade.*

which prevented them from establishing a footing as quickly as the centre regiments who were now pushing on into the enclosure in the teeth of a biting fire from both infantry and artillery.

Thus the attack of the Highland Brigade had taken on the form of a wedge with flanks held back and centre going forward to the inner lines of entrenchments, from the southern end of which

Private of the Black Watch. He wears the 'valise' pattern equipment with haversack and water bottle. (Michael Roffe)

intense fire made it impossible to advance over the open ground; only at the northern inner face could any headway be made and then only in the face of stubborn opposition.

The Attack of Graham's Brigade

On the right, starting more than ten minutes after the Highlanders' attacking time of 5.20 a.m., General Graham personally led his brigade to the ditch and parapet before them. On the brigade's right flank, the Royal Irish, taking up successive positions, advanced at a rush against a parapet

▲ Graham's Brigade of Willis's 1st Division attacking a gun position in the Egyptian lines, on the right of the British attack. This graphic sketch was produced on the spot by the eminent Victorian War artist R. Caton Woodville.

▶ Sweeping around the enemy left flank and rear, the Cavalry Division took numerous prisoners – in the manner of this sketch by the R. Caton Woodville, showing a trooper of the Household Cavalry capturing a very frightened Egyptian infantryman.

slightly lower than in other places, but still pouring out a heavy fire. The Yorks & Lancs moved forward in a single rush upon the work and parapet to their front, carrying it just before the Royal Irish Fusiliers entered on its southern aspect. The Royal Marines, who had not fired a shot until within 100 yards of their parapet, seized and held it, the enemy sullenly withdrawing and stubbornly holding their ground in a formed body some 50 feet back, as they did all along the Brigade front. But time and the coming of daylight brought reinforcements to the two attacking infantry brigades.

The Cavalry and Artillery in Action

At 4.40 a.m., on the extreme right, the cavalry advanced at a slow walk, then a trot until, at about 4.55 when about 2,000 yards from the enemy position, they heard the first shots and increased their pace, until they came under fire from a work on the Egyptian left. The Royal Horse Artillery galloped forward and silenced this fort, as well as a field battery on the open ground in rear of the parapet. With the Indian Brigade leading, in line of squadron columns, the cavalry passed the line of entrenchments and began to swing round on to the left-rear of the enemy; this was at about the same time as the infantry brigades were beginning to drive back the still resisting Egyptian infantry.

It was at this moment that a party of Black Watch entered the rear of an artillery emplacement on their extreme right, from which guns were firing into the rear of Graham's infantry, and shot down the gunners at their work. This allowed a battery of Wolseley's artillery to be manhandled up the parapet south of the emplacement and come into action. At the same time, other British guns came into action directly in front of the parapet. On the approach-march, made in echelon of brigade-divisions, the artillery had been halted at 4.50 when the advancing Highlanders were seen to be overlapping their front; then the enemy artillery opened fire and the British guns, being too exposed on the sky-line, dismounted drivers and remained halted until the light improved. At about 5.20 a.m. three guns had penetrated the enemy lines and were firing to their left on the enemy facing the Highlanders, with two more guns enfilading the Egyptians to the north.

Gunner of N/2 Battery, Royal Artillery, with rammer/sponge. (Pierre Turner)

Also at about the same time, British batteries on the right came into action, outside the ditch, against that sector of the enemy lines holding out to the north, which had not been assailed by infantry.

From 5.30 to 6 a.m. Graham's Brigade pushed forward steadily upon formed masses of enemy beyond the captured parapet, who were under fire from Horse Artillery on their left, two guns on their right, more guns to their right-front, and threatened by cavalry in their left-rear. It was not surprising that they quickly gave way, to become a mass of fugitives, retarding the cavalry advance towards the bridge of Tel el-Kebir. The Guards Brigade, after advancing steadily upon the parapet, wheeled left to follow Graham's men, now sweeping down on enemy lines in front of the bridge. During this period all resistance ceased in the northern half of the enemy position.

At 5.20 a.m. the Highland Brigade on the British left, exposed to fierce fire from many direc-

tions, broke into detached parties of from 60 to 300 men led by officers of all regiments, to advance by rushes over the ground between the first and second lines of entrenchments, and along the ditch. The Egyptian infantry held out resolutely at each turn of the parapet, embrasure and traverse. The Highlanders were greatly aided by the three guns which had been brought into the lines, their shrapnel fire at 1,000 yards' range proving very effective in silencing fire from the inner entrenchments. On the extreme left of the attack the Highland Light Infantry, reinforced by part of 4 Brigade, again attacked and carried the defences facing them, then

▲ *Having been unable to penetrate the Egyptian position, the Highland Light Infantry (on the British left) again attacked and carried the defences; sweeping down southwards towards the canal, they carried the remainder of the works on that side.*

sweeping down southwards towards the canal, carried the remainder of the works on that side.

At 6 a.m. the Egyptian right was still fighting although being steadily pushed back; but on their left (the northern flank) a broken mass of fugitives was being driven in full flight by the cavalry and horse artillery. At this time, the advanced elements

▲ British artillerymen forcing their way over the parapet of the Egyptian lines at Tel el-Kebir. Highlanders can be seen in the picture, so these must be the guns brought into action on the British left where The Black Watch had silenced an enemy battery, allowing the British guns to come into action against the enemy facing the High-landers, and also to enfilade Egyptian forces in the other half of the lines. (From the painting by John Charlton)

▶ The Highland Light Infantry had a difficult time crossing the ditch and scaling the parapet, but eventually succeeded and are here shown fighting their way over the open ground within.

of the Highland Brigade – about 200 men of all three regiments – appeared above the enemy camp, with a full sight of the mass of fugitives and reserves struggling to make their escape. Hamley ordered Alison to advance upon the camp, which was duly captured, and to move on the bridge and railway station. On the tow-path of the canal beyond the railway station he finally called a halt; Sir Garnet Wolseley, who earlier had advanced into the lines with his Staff, rode forward and reached the bridge at Tel el-Kebir at the same time as the Highlanders.

General Macpherson's India Contingent marched in fours over the restricted ground south of the canal with the cavalry in the rear; they had covered three miles when the noise of battle reached them. The Naval Brigade was moving on the north bank, both forces using the tow-path whose banks served them as a protecting traverse; communication was maintained by RE pontoons on the canal keeping abreast of them. When they were fired on by enemy guns in pits ahead of the force, the Seaforth Highlanders were pushed forward against the guns and about 400 infantry in trenches; simultaneously the Mountain Battery came into action from the top of the banks, firing at the gun flashes. The Seaforths advanced in rushes, firing volleys at intervals and well-supported by the Naval Gatlings on the north bank; then they fixed bayonets and charged, while the 20th Native Infantry took the battery in flank; both were supported by the two other Indian Regiments.

At about 6 a.m. the enemy were driven from their positions and four guns were captured; a defended village was taken, and the whole line advanced, driving the broken enemy before them, and capturing his guns.

Discussing the battle after his capture, Arabi claimed that the defeat was caused by the precipitous flight of his left flank, the sector on his right attacked by the Highlanders being only involved in the general confusion when they were overwhelmed by fugitives from the left. In his opinion his intact reserve's retreat, allied to the general attempts to escape to the station, undoubtedly began before the Highlanders came on the scene, and were caused by the cavalry's advance and the threatening appearance of the British 1st Division in the distance.

The Egyptian infantry at Tel el-Kebir were said to have borne the unexpected attack out of the darkness with the discipline and desperation of first-class troops; the Highlanders, suffering 243 of the 339 casualties sustained by Wolseley's force, encountered strong resistance from the Egyptian Guard Regiment which fell back silently and sullenly before them. Commanding the Highland Brigade, Sir Archibald Alison said, 'I must do justice to those much maligned Egyptian soldiers. I never saw men

◀ *N/A Troop, Royal Horse Artillery, equipped with 9pdr or 13pdr guns, surmounting the ditch and parapet during the final stages of the action.*

▼ *Egyptian infantry surrendering to the 13th Bengal Lancers, leading the British cavalry advance around the Egyptian left-rear at Tel el-Kebir. Drawn by R. Caton Woodville from a sketch by an on-the-spot war artist.*

▶ *Immediately after the charge of the Highlanders the attack became general, and the enemy were forced to evacuate their trenches. Meanwhile the British cavalry had worked round the Egyptian left and the India Contingent had reached a bridge over the canal in the rear, ready to cut down the fugitives. The result was that by six o'clock in the morning the battle was won.*

fight more steadily. They were falling-back on an inner line of works which we had taken in flank and at every re-entering angle, at every battery and redoubt, they rallied and renewed the fight. Five or six times we had to close on them with the bayonet and I saw those poor men fighting hard when their officers were flying before us.' It was mostly the black Nubian infantry who fought well; hitherto stationed at Damietta whence they came to reinforce Tel el-Kebir, they were considered by many to be the best troops Arabi had, with finer physiques than the *fellahin*, and they were better shots, their eyes were unaffected by the chronic ophthalmia of the Egyptians. Tel el-Kebir showed that while Egyptian soldiers were unable to meet Wolseley's men in open fighting, they were by no means to be despised when fighting from defensive positions.

The Pursuit and the Drive for Cairo

Straight over the battlefield without halting, the India Contingent went in hot pursuit and that afternoon occupied Zagazig, to break communications between the various elements of the Egyptian Army dispersed throughout the Delta. Cutting through the fleeing enemy, the bulk of the Cavalry Division and the Mounted Infantry had reached Belbeis by mid-afternoon and occupied the place.

At 4.30 a.m. on 14 September the cavalry advance on Cairo began. They halted some miles distant from the Abbassiyeh Barracks on the eastern

Private of the Royal Marine Light Infantry. (Michael Roffe)

◀ *Top left: in his camp at Tel el-Kebir, Arabi Pasha, the Egyptian commander, had a palatial tent in which he was sleeping at the time of the British attack, being woken by the sound of the firing. By the time he had dressed his army was in full retreat, so he made his escape with them. When the camp was taken 1st Division's commander General Willis, and his staff, took over the tent.*

◀ *Below left: Scene outside the field hospital at Tel el-Kebir. This drawing by Melton Prior conveys something of the dire situation in which soldiers wounded in the colonial wars found themselves,*

lying out in the sun for hours until taken into the stifling confines of the surgical tent for perhaps the most painful hours of their lives.

▼ *Highland Light Infantry guard Egyptian prisoners of war, taken in the area on the extreme right of their line. Drawn by F. F. Weedon, special war artist of* **The Illustrated London News.**

side of the city, and Lieutenant-Colonel Herbert Stewart went forward with about 50 cavalrymen. As this force approached the barracks, a party of Egyptian cavalry with white flags tied to their carbines came out to meet them. Learning that Arabi had galloped off alone from the field on a swift horse and was at his house in Cairo, a force was sent into the city and arrived there at 4.30 p.m. The citadel surrendered its 6,000-strong garrison; and shortly afterwards Arabi Pasha and Toulba Pasha surrendered themselves unconditionally.

There seems to have been no computation made of the Egyptian casualties, but it was said at the time by those present that they were considerable, causing surprise that so many men could have been slain in such a short time. They were said to have been lying dead in hundreds where the Highlanders had broken into the entrenchments, and large numbers of dead were scattered along their line of retreat. The correspondent of *The Standard* estimated 2,500 to 3,000 dead; another source reckoned 1,500 to

2,000. The sufferings of the many wounded was also remarked upon, despite whatever efforts could be made by British medical personnel.

By 10 a.m. next day Sir Garnet Wolseley and his Staff, with an escort of Guards, arrived in Cairo by train; the city was rapidly occupied by a large British force. Egyptian military positions and forces at Kafr ed-Dauar and elsewhere in the Delta surrendered without any resistance.

The war was over.

British Losses at Tel el-Kebir

	Killed		Wounded		Missing	
	Officers	Men	Officers	Men	Officers	Men
Staff			2			
19th Hussars			1			
Royal Artillery			2	17		
Grenadier Guards		1	1	9		
Coldstream Guards			1	7		
Scots Guards				4		
Royal Highlanders	2	7	6	39		2
Gordon Highlanders	1	5	1	29		4
Cameron Highlanders		13	3	45		
Highland Light Infantry	3	14	5	52		
2nd Royal Irish	1	1	2	17		
York and Lancaster				12		
1st Royal Irish Fusiliers		2		34		3
Royal Marine Light Infantry	2	3	1	53		21
DCLI			1	5		
King's Royal Ride Corps				20		
India Contingent		1		9		
Seaforth Highlanders		1		3		
Chaplains			1			
Total	9	48	27	356		30

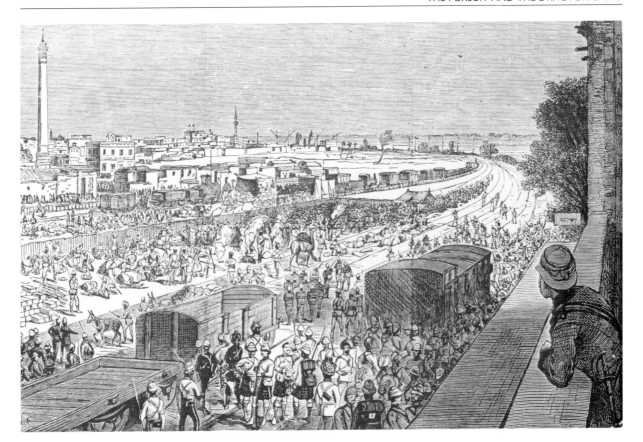

▲ *The town of Zagazig, midway between Tel el-Kebir and Cairo, was first occupied by the India Contingent on the afternoon of the battle. They went straight through the battlefield to secure the town. Later, as can be seen from the sketch, the entire army seems to have used it as a staging-post on their route to Cairo.*

◀ *Highland Brigade casualties at Tel el-Kebir, waiting at the railway station to be taken to hospital.*

▶ *The Citadel in Cairo surrendered to British advance forces on 14 September.*

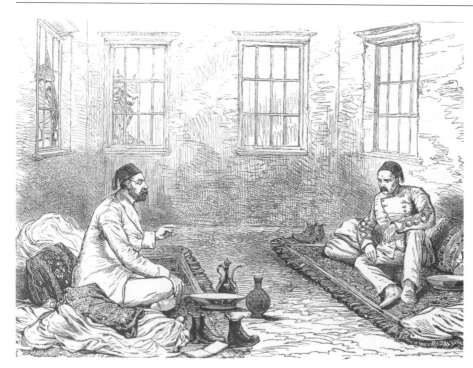

◄ *The room in the Abbassieh Barracks in Cairo where Arabi Pasha and his subordinate Toulba Pasha were held after their surrender to the British in the evening of 14 September 1882, the day after the battle at Tel el-Kebir.*

▼ *After the War in Egypt had ended there was a Grand Review of the victors in Cairo before the Khedive. Here the Baluchis are marching past.*

IN SUMMATION

It was said at the time that seldom had a campaign been more completely successful or more creditable to a leader and his troops. Striking a familiar note, one writer felt that 'the war looked more like a game of *Kriegsspiel* than a stern reality, so precise, so careful, were the plans and calculations of Sir Garnet Wolseley, and so punctually did he carry out the scheme he had matured before leaving London'. Another military correspondent of the day said, 'He

was correct almost to a day as to the date on which the campaign would be over. Not only has he finished the war triumphantly, but he has left no loose threads to be taken up. He has not merely defeated the insurgents, but he has burnt up the insurrection, leaving no pestiferous and harassing dregs behind. His strategy and tactics have been able and masterly. Instead of – as an ordinary general would have done – trying an advance from Alexandria, after previously capturing the Aboukir ports and Kafr ed-Dauar, he bemused the enemy in front of Alexandria, and then, deceiving everyone, including his own generals he, by an admirable series of combinations, in concert with the Navy, seized the Canal, and transferred his base to Ismailia. When there, instead of a rapid and showy dash into the

▼ The final scenes at the trial in Cairo on 3 December 1882 of Arabi Pasha, defeated commander of the Egyptian forces and former Minister of War. At this point he was sentenced to death but this was immediately commuted to life exile in Ceylon, according to a prior arrangement with his captors.

heart of the country, which might have succeeded, but would have involved great risk, much loss of life, and would have won him only a first victory, to be followed by a prolonged campaign, he decided to wait until he had matured all his arrangements for one crushing blow, which should end the campaign.'

History has to be consulted to determine whether Arabi was a pure-minded patriot labouring for the nationalization of his country; an unscrupulous and ambitious mutineer aiming at taking the country over from the Khedive; or a mere tool of the Sultan of Turkey in his aim of restoring full Turkish power in Egypt. Whatever the truth of the matter, it cannot be denied that Arabi was a man of great determination, as shown by what he accomplished in his country in a very short time; his relatively rapid downfall was only brought about by the intensive effort of raising a major expeditionary force by the sole major power unwilling to allow the rise of a dictator likely to affect its interests.

After his defeat at Tel el-Kebir, Arabi Pasha and his closest associates were brought to trial on 3 December 1882. After an arrangement had been agreed, they received death sentences that were immediately commuted to life exile in Ceylon. Arabi spent eighteen years there until pardoned in 1903 when he was permitted to return to Egypt, where he died of cancer in 1911.

◀ *Queen Victoria presents decorations to soldiers of the Egyptian expedition at Windsor Castle; from* **The Illustrated London News** *of 2 December 1882.*

Battle Honours and Awards

These Regiments were authorized by GO32/1883 to add 'EGYPT 1882' to their Colours and appointments:

British Army
1st Life Guards
2nd Life Guards
Royal Horse Guards
4th Dragoon Guards
7th Dragoon Guards
Grenadier Guards
Coldstream Guards
Scots Guards
The Royal Irish Regiment
The Duke of Cornwall's Light Infantry
The Royal Sussex Regiment
The South Staffordshire Regiment
The Sherwood Foresters
The Royal Berkshire Regiment
The Queen's Own (Royal West Kent Regiment)
The King's (Shropshire Light Infantry)
The Manchester Regiment
The Highland Light Infantry
The Seaforth Highlanders
The Queen's Own Cameron Highlanders
8th (City of London) Bn, The London Regiment (Post Office Rifles)
19th Hussars
The Black Watch
The King's Royal Rifle Corps
The York and Lancaster Regiment
The Gordon Highlanders
The Royal Irish Fusiliers

Indian Army
2nd Regiment of Bengal Cavalry
6th Regiment of Bengal Cavalry
13th Regiment of Bengal Lancers
Queen's Own Corps of Sappers & Miners
7th Regiment, Bengal Native Infantry
20th (Punjab) Regiment, Bengal Native Infantry
29th Regiment, Bombay Native Infantry or 2nd Baluch Battalion

The following Regiments were authorized to bear 'TEL-EL-KEBIR' as a battle honour:

British Army
1st Life Guards
2nd Life Guards
Royal Horse Guards
4th Dragoon Guards
7th Dragoon Guards
19th Hussars
Grenadier Guards
Coldstream Guards
Scots Guards
The Royal Irish Regiment
The Duke of Cornwall's Light Infantry
The Black Watch
The King's Royal Rifle Corps
The York and Lancaster Regiment
The Highland Light Infantry
The Seaforth Highlanders
The Gordon Highlanders
The Queen's Own Cameron Highlanders
The Royal Irish Fusiliers

Indian Army
2nd Regiment of Bengal Cavalry
6th Regiment of Bengal Cavalry
13th Regiment of Bengal Lancers
Queen's Own Corps of Sappers & Miners
7th Regiment, Bengal Native Infantry
20th (Punjab) Regiment, Bengal Native Infantry
29th Regiment, Bombay Native Infantry or 2nd Baluch Battalion

The above battle honour commemorates the first action in which the Household Cavalry were engaged since Waterloo, sixty-seven years before.

A total of forty-three British and Indian Army units took part in the campaign, but only a relatively small number of them received the 'EGYPT' medal with bar 'TEL-EL-KEBIR'; the number of such medals and bars awarded to Indian Army personnel is uncertain. For example, 2nd Manchester Regiment were present in Egypt, but none were authorized to wear the bar. Only one company of the Royal West Kent Regiment received the bar; and the following received the medal less the bar - 1st Royal Sussex Regiment; 1st South Staffordshire Regiment; 1st Berkshire Regiment; 1st King's (Shropshire Light Infantry); and the Sherwood Forresters.
    In addition to those regiments granted the Battle Honour

'Tel-El-Kebir', and this includes three squadrons each of the 1st and 2nd Life Guards, Royal Horse Guards, 4th Dragoon Guards and 7th Dragoon Guards, and one squadron 19th Hussars, the following units received the EGYPT Medal with Bar:

Batteries 'A', 'C', 'D', 'F', 'G', 'H', 'I', 'J' and 'N' Royal Artillery; 7th Mountain Battery, Royal Artillery; 4/1 and 5/1 London, and 5/1 and 6/1 Scottish Divisions Royal Artillery.
Royal Marine Artillery; 26th Company, Royal Engineers; The Royal Naval Brigade; The Army Hospital Corps; The Malta Auxiliary Transport.

Every officer and man who took part in the campaign received the Khedive of Egypt's Commemorative Bronze Star.

During the Crimean War British officers and soldiers were authorized to wear decorations and medals bestowed by our allies; acting upon this precedence, Queen Victoria sanctioned the acceptance of Orders of the Osmanieh and the Medjidieh from the Sultan of Turkey, bestowed as follows:

	Osmanieh	Medjidieh
General officers	4	6
Staff officers	51	94
1st Life Guards (one squadron)	1	-
2nd Life Guards (one squadron)	1	1
Royal Horse Guards (one squadron)	-	1
4th Dragoon Guards	-	3
7th Dragoon Guards	2	1

CHRONOLOGY

1879
26 June Tewfik becomes Khedive of Egypt
1881
1 February Egyptian Army mutiny
9 September Palace confrontation between Khedive and Arabi. Ministers resign office.
1882
January Arabi appointed Minister for War
March Arabi made a Pasha
April Circassian officers, plotting to kill Arabi, are arrested and tried. Court-martialled, their punishments drastically reduced by the Khedive.
5 May French propose that six English and six French warships be sent to Alexandria.
15 May The combined fleet leaves Suda in Crete
20 May The fleet arrives at Alexandria. The Egyptian Ministry resigns in a body, protesting against foreign interference.
21 May Arabi Pasha holds a demonstration, demanding to be reinstated as Minister of War.
26-7 May Egyptian soldiers attack Europeans and threaten to storm Alexandria.
28 May Arabi Pasha becomes virtual dictator. Orders Alexandria forts to be put in state of defensive readiness, despite contrary orders from Khedive and British Admiral.
11 June Massacre of Europeans in Alexandria.
7 July Admiral Seymour threatens bombardment if defensive work does not cease.
10 July 24-hour ultimatum sent by Admiral Seymour. Last Europeans leave Alexandria. French withdraw their warships.
11 July British fleet bombards Alexandria forts.
12 July Egyptian soldiers and Bedouin sack Alexandria.
13 July Alexandria on fire. Arabi and his forces withdraw outside city.
14 July Naval landing-parties go ashore. Rescue Khedive who had been threatened by armed soldiers.

15 July Sailors and Marines go through city suppressing marauders.
17 July *Tamar* (bringing Royal Marines), *Agincourt* and *Northumberland* arrive, bringing South Staffordshire Regiment and King's Royal Rifle Corps. General Sir Archibald Alison arrives from England, takes command of this force.
22 July Discovers Arabi's force entrenched at Kafr ed-Dauar. First skirmishes occur.
23 July *Malabar* arrives bringing Duke of Cornwall's Light Infantry and a wing of the 38th. These join Alison's force and move out to occupy Ramleh.
24 July Contact made with Arabi and the two forces confront each other, within artillery range, in hastily fortified positions.
25 July In England the Army Reserve is called-up.
30 July Brigade of Guards leaves England.
2 August General Sir Garnet Wolseley leaves England.
3 August Marines from the fleet occupy Suez.
5 August A reconnaissance-in-force, including armoured train, moves over area Ramleh – Kafr ed-Dauar. Engages and defeats enemy force at Mahalla Junction.
6 August General Graham takes command of British position at Ramleh.
8 August Troops from India arrive at Suez, others and units from Britain continue arriving during next two weeks.
10 August Duke of Connaught, with Chief-of-Staff Sir John Adye, arrive at Alexandria.
12 August Brigade of Guards arrives at Alexandria.
15 August Sir Garnet Wolseley arrives at Alexandria. Two infantry divisions, plus cavalry, artillery and Staff Corps, leave Britain. Mounted Infantry, under Captain Parr, carry out reconnaissance towards enemy positions; minor engagement ensues.
16 August General Wolseley, Sir Evelyn Wood and

Sir Edward Hamley, accompanied by the Duke of Connaught and other generals, inspect British positions, and view Arabi's formidable entrenchments.

17 August Orders issued for troops to prepare to embark. Units of 1st Division that have landed re-embark.

18 August Work of embarkation goes on.

19 August Ships sail from Alexandria for Ismailia. Considerable enemy activity, with firing, in front of British position at Ramleh.

20 August General Sir Evelyn Wood sends Berkshire Regiment out on a reconnaissance. Port Said occupied.

21 August General Sir Edward Hamley sends out the Black Watch on a reconnaissance towards Kafr ed-Dauar. Fleet off Ismailia, embarkation begins. Last of British Expeditionary Force lands at Alexandria. Sir Garnet Wolseley and Admiral Seymour at Ismailia. Nefisha occupied by General Graham. General McPherson, commanding India Contingent, with his Staff, arrives at Suez

22 August Graham takes a strong force towards Ramses, Magfar and Tel el-Maskhuta; engages enemy throughout day.

23 August Opposed advance continues.

25 August General advance against Tel el-Maskhuta begins; found to be deserted. Drury Lowe, with cavalry, makes wide circuit and takes Mahsama. Force encamps at both places.

26 August General Graham takes and occupies Kassassin.

27 August Mahmoud Pasha Fehmy, Arabi's Chief-of-Staff, falls into British hands.

28 August Battle of Kassassin. Infantry of the Indian Division, with artillery and commissariat corps, lands at Ismailia 28–31 August.

29 August Orders received at Alexandria for the Highland Brigade, under General Alison, and General Sir Edward Hamley and Staff, to embark for Ismailia. Sir Evelyn Wood remains in charge of the city and lines at Ramleh.

30 August The force embarks; sails on 31st, arriving Port Said 1 September. Remain in transports off Ismailia until 9 September, then land and march to Kassassin, arriving 13 September.

5 September War Office in London issue orders for dispatch of 4,000 more troops from Great Britain.

6 September Egyptian force reconnoitres British positions at Kassassin.

7 September Indian cavalry and Mounted Infantry make close reconnaissance of Egyptian lines at Tel el-Kebir. General Willis and Staff arrive at Kassassin, as does General Drury Lowe and the cavalry; Guards on their way there.

8 September Strong British reconnaissance of south bank of canal and adjacent area.

9 September Arabi personally present at strong Egyptian reconnaissance of British position at Kassassin. Egyptian attack on Kassassin beaten off.

11–12 September General Sir Garnet Wolseley and other senior officers reconnoitre both sides of enemy's position. Royal Irish Fusiliers(87th) and Pontoon Train arrive in camp.

13 September Battle of Tel el-Kebir. Defeated Arabi flees to Cairo. Indian Cavalry and Household Cavalry pursue fleeing Egyptian Army, arriving at Belbeis in evening.

14 September This cavalry force arrives at Abbassiah Barracks outside Cairo in early evening. Town and garrison of Cairo surrender. Egyptians at Kafr ed-Dauar make overtures for the surrender of the position.

15 September Finding lines at Kafr ed-Dauar abandoned, British troops from Ramleh take possession. Via the re-established telegraphic communications system, Arabi and his officers offer submission to the Khedive, who refuses to accept them. General Sir Garnet Wolseley enters Cairo.

17 September General Sir Evelyn Wood and Staff enter lines of Kafr ed-Dauar. Arabi Pasha a prisoner in Cairo.

18 September Egyptian garrison of the Aboukir Forts march to Kafr ed-Dauar and surrender. Egyptian force at Tantah surrenders to Seaforth Highlanders.

20 September The Khedive, escorted by Bengal Lancers, drives through Alexandria.

25 September Khedive leaves for Cairo.

27 September Special Commission appointed by Khedive to consider all acts performed by civil and military persons during the rebellion. Arabi and his followers to be court-martialled.

30 September Great Review and March Past of British troops in Cairo.

2 October Valentine Baker Pasha arrives in Cairo

from Constantinople; has audience with Khedive concerning re-organization of Egyptian Army.

5 October Arabi Pasha and Toulba Pasha handed over to Egyptian Government, brought before court and charged with treason.

20 October Horse Guards return to London, disembark at West India Docks.

21 October March through streets to Albany Barracks. Life Guards arrive home and march through City on following day. Royal Marines land at Portsmouth. Four hundred officers and men receive from the Queen at Windsor the Egypt Medal announced in a General Order on 17 October 1882.

18 November Great Review of troops marching through London before the Queen.

A GUIDE TO FURTHER READING

The following books were used as reference when compiling this book:

ARCHER, Thomas. *The War in Egypt and the Soudan*, vol. 1, 1886

FARWELL, Byron. *Queen Victoria's Little Wars*, 1973

FEATHERSTONE, Donald. *Colonial Small Wars, 1837-1901*, 1973

— *Victoria's Enemies*, 1989: *Weapons and Equipment of the Victorian Soldier*, 1978

FIELD, Colonel C. *Britain's Sea Soldiers*, 1924

Leslie, N.B. *The Battle Honours of the British and Indian Armies, 1695-1914*, 1970

MAURICE, John Frederick. *Military History of the Campaign of 1882 in Egypt*, 1887

SANDES, Lieutenant-Colonel E.W.C. *The Royal Engineers in Egypt and the Sudan*, 1937

TOPPEL, Don, and WAHL, Paul. *The Gatling Gun*, 1965

WOLSELEY, Field Marshal Viscount. *Story of a Soldier's Life*, 1903

The Illustrated London News for the year 1882

The Graphic for the year 1882

WARGAMING THE EGYPTIAN WAR OF 1882

Being ambitious men of broad vision, wargamers dream of refighting history's famous battles, of reproducing a realistic Waterloo on a tabletop terrain measuring perhaps 8 feet by 6 feet – the result may bear the name and a slight resemblance, but precious little else. For Waterloo, although a relatively small battle for the numbers involved, stretched across a frontage of about four miles and involved nearly 200,000 French, British, Prussians, Dutch, Belgians, etc., which means a mighty lot of scaling-down, both in men and ground! However, military history abounds with smaller, more suitable battles and campaigns where the size of the armies allows realistic scaling-down – essential because if the battle is to bear anything more than a titular resemblance to its real-life counterpart, the tabletop armies must conform to an accurate proportion of the forces involved, both in numbers and types.

So the sensible wargamer seeks suitable 'small wars' that are well documented, have maps available, involve relatively small numbers and limited objectives, and whose battlefields lend themselves to miniature reproduction. Many 'small wars' were also short wars which means that the entire campaign can be refought, using area-maps upon which the protagonists plot their moves – and there can be no time when the wargamer feels more like a real-life commander than when studying a spread-out map, aware that he has the power to manoeuvre whole armies across its contours, to destroy the enemy gathering on a similar map marked by his opponent.

In its overall context, the operations in Egypt in 1882 would seem to represent a true 'small war' ready-and-waiting to be wargamed, and indeed justifies the attempt while, at the same time, possessing certain snags. For example, on paper it was a conflict between two trained and disciplined armies, organized in battalions, squadrons and batteries, both employing similar weapons of the time – but

with Arabi's Egyptian troops emulating, vainly except so far as courage was concerned, those well-tried systems and methods employed by the British in regular warfare. To the British, it was a not unwelcome and certainly easier style of fighting than that required in recent affairs against fierce Ashantis in their dense forests, militaristic Zulus in South Africa, or warrior-hillmen on the North-West Frontier of India and in Afghanistan. In this current conflict in Egypt, both sides 'knew what to expect' so far as formations and tactics were concerned, which made it more or less a regular, 'civilized' war – at which the British were far more practised than their *fellahin* opponents.

So, although it will make an 'organized wargame', this undoubted inequality requires rules and game-conditions to reflect it on the table-top; the other necessary factor is 'unbalanced' forces, the Egyptians fielding larger numbers to compensate for their morale and tactical inadequacies. However, this is already present through the real-life numbers on both sides who actually contested the battles – at Tel el-Kebir, the Egyptians with modern artillery emplaced in strong well-prepared fortifications outnumbered their British attackers with 25-30,000 men and 75 guns against 17,400 men with 61 guns and six Gatlings – for the type of battle, these odds could well have been reversed.

From a campaign point of view, he who dons the mantle of Arabi Pasha will, with hindsight, not be so blind as to leave his army in one part of the country while Wolseley sails round to his rear – and that is the key to it all! This might make it preferable to commence your Egyptian War at the point where Wolseley marches out of Ismailia towards Kassassin. And frankly, the battles could be bettered – it is not going to be easy to march a wargames army unseen throughout the night to attack an historically unsuspecting Arabi, when he who wears his hat knows perfectly well what happened on 12/13 September

1882. Anyway, attacks by numerically inferior wargames armies on superior numbers behind strong fortifications are not likely to encourage the friendship and goodwill which forms the principal boon of the hobby! The action at Kassassin on 28 August has certain promising aspects, if both wargamers adhere to a pre-designed time-chart – but then it becomes a demonstration of what truly occurred rather than a competitive game where the best tactician wins – with a bit of dice luck!

Probably Graham's operations in the Tel el-Maskhuta area on 26 August will make the best wargame and is definitely worth trying; read it first in greater detail than possible here – say in Colonel Maurice's book (*see* 'A Guide to Further Reading') and then, having been sufficiently stimulated, set it up on the tabletop battlefield.

Finally, reverting to wargaming difficulties arising from re-creating Tel el-Kebir, one man who did it with great style was American artist Robert Andrew Parker who, in the November 1963 issue of no less a magazine than *Esquire*, posed a selection of photographs of the battle, using Britain's 54mm model soldiers – in the manner of H. G. Wells in his immortal book *Little Wars*.